Those of Distant Campfires

Those of Distant Campfires

The Unconquered Seminoles

Dr. Sandi Towers

Writers Club Press
San Jose New York Lincoln Shanghai

Those of Distant Campfires
The Unconquered Seminoles

Writers Club Press
an imprint of iUniverse, Inc.

For information address:
iUniverse, Inc.
5220 S. 16th St., Suite 200
Lincoln, NE 68512
www.iuniverse.com

ISBN: 0-595-20620-4

Printed in the United States of America

Contents

List of Illustrations

Cover Photo

A Seminole Indian Dwelling, circa 1884. Reproduced from the Florida Photographic Collection, Florida State Archives.

Chapter Six

Map of Florida of the First Seminole War's historic points.

Chapter Seven

Coacoochee (Wild Cat), from a negative from P.K. Yonge Library. Reproduced from the Florida Photographic Collection, Florida State Archives.

Gopher John (John Cavallo) from John T. Sprague's The Origin, Progress and Conclusion of the Florida War, New York Appleton, circa 1848. Reproduced from the Florida Photographic Collection, Florida State Archives.

Portrait of Osceola, circa 1838, Color Oil, 29"X24", The National Portrait Gallery, Smithsonian Institution, Washington, D.C. Reproduced from the Florida Photographic Collection, Florida State Archives.

Chapter Eight

Drawing of Seminole Chief Billy Bowlegs, circa 1858. Reproduced from the Florida Photographic Collection, Florida State Archives.

Map of Florida of the Second Seminole War's historic points.

Chapter Nine

Map of Indian Territory.

Chapter Eleven

Map of Florida of the Third Seminole War's historic points.

Acknowledgements

I wish to thank Lorene Gopher of the Cultural and Educational Program for the Seminole Tribe of Florida for her help with some of the pronunciations in this book.

I want to thank my husband Dale for producing the maps of Florida and Oklahoma for the book, and for his assistance with the book's graphics.

I also want to thank Mary Reynolds Lamary, my editor, for her patience, assistance, and invaluable input into this book.

Introduction

The Seminoles and their ancestors inhabited the peninsula of Florida for some 12,000-15,000 years before the arrival of the white man. The true story of their forcible removal and the related deceptions in connection with that removal are embarrassing and unacceptable events in the history the United States.

In this cybernetic age, as we seek peace and alternatives to conflicts, we can learn by the study and research of Seminole customs how to accomplish these goals. The culture of the Seminoles illustrates their belief in humankind, nature, nonviolence, and the acceptance of blacks into their society. The Seminoles in particular with their matrilineal and egalitarian culture exemplified a strong and fair value system. Their spirituality further supported their humanitarian beliefs.

The removal of the Seminoles from Florida to Oklahoma represents the avarice of the US Government and settlers coming into Florida. The author views the Seminole resistance to their removal to a foreign and forbidding new land as totally just. The attempt by other cultures to interfere with the Seminole practice of acceptance of blacks into their culture is seen as unjust by the author. Prior to the middle of the 20th Century, the white man was consumed only with political and economic goals in the settlement of the New World.

"Our nation was born in genocide when it embraced the doctrine that the original American, the Indian, was an inferior race. Even before there were large numbers of Negroes on our shores, the scar of racial hatred had already disfigured colonial society. From the sixteenth century forward, blood flowed in battles over racial supremacy. We are perhaps the only nation which tried as a matter of national policy to wipe out its indigenous population." (From-*Why We Can't Wait*-Martin Luther King, Jr.)

Mary Reynolds Lamary, Editor

CHAPTER ONE
Ancient Florida

Florida some 30 million years ago was merely a series of low sandy islands rising out of the shallow waters of the Gulf of Mexico. As the polar ice caps grew and water levels lowered these islands grew in size, finally growing together and joining the North American continent. With exposure to sun and warmth vegetation and animal life began to flourish. During four geologic epochs Florida's landmass would shrink and grow according to the world's climate. Forests would establish themselves then give way to grasslands when drier and more arid times would come. Florida's animal life would also change according to the climate; Florida was a place of abundant life. Yet there were no humans.

Some 40,000 to 15,000 years ago, at the end of the Pleistocene (PLYS-to-seen) Epoch glaciers covered much of the earth. At this time a land bridge opened from Siberia to Alaska. Humans began to follow prey across this land bridge moving more and more east and south. They entered the Rocky Mountains in the western US, and gradually spread throughout the North and South American continent.

The first Native Americans came to Florida some 12,000 years ago. The land they found was far different than the land we know today. It was the end of the Great Ice Age, and Florida was cooler and drier. The oceans were much lower than they are now, since huge amounts of water were tied up in glaciers. Sea level was as much as 300 feet below where it is today. Florida of 12,000 years ago was twice its present size.

Yet this land the first people of Florida found offered a much gentler climate than the rest of North America. The Florida peninsula stretching down toward the warm waters of the Caribbean offered the first inhabitants winters without severe freezes, and mild summers. Summers were much cooler than the present Florida summers.

Because so much water was tied up in the glaciers of the north, Florida was actually an arid place. There was a lack of drinkable ground water since the sea level was so low. Adding to these arid conditions was the fact rainfall was less than today. So most ponds or lakes were rarely full.

There were a few forests of oak and hickory, where water had collected, but most of Florida was covered by drought resistant grasses and scrub oak. The rivers that existed were more like dry streambeds with the occasional sinkhole. These sinkholes were the only available fresh water. Along the Gulf and Atlantic coasts there were salt marshes.

Ice Age animals still flourished in Florida when the first people arrived. The grasslands were home to now extinct species of horse, bison, camel, and mammoth. In dry areas there were giant armadillos and land tortoises. Mastodons, tapirs, and ground sloth were found in woods and marshes. There were capybaras and beavers in the few lakes and ponds. Preying on all of these were the carnivores, i.e., saber tooth cat, huge lions, and giant dire wolves.

The Florida ecology also boasted the usual array of fish, amphibians, reptiles, and birds. Most of these species were larger then. There were manatees, otters, and muskrats in the rivers. Deer, rabbit, black bear, raccoon, opossum, panther, bobcat and other small mammals populated the land. To exist in Pleistocene Florida, the first settlers had to be skillful hunters. They needed to be proficient hunters for both large and small game, and they needed to have an extensive knowledge of various plant foods that were available.

These first settlers—the Paleoindians needed water to survive. Because water was so scarce the Paleoindians settled where they found water. The same deep sinkholes attracted animals as well. The most consistent sources of water were found in the north of the state since more water catchments were found there because of the limestone geology. This is what drew the Paleoindians into the region.

These watering holes were places where the Paleoindians camped, and sites where animals could be ambushed and caught. Today these campsites are found at the bottom of rivers and sinkholes. What has been found at these "underwater" campsites is quite remarkable. Paleoindian tools and animal bones of extinct species are found together. This is evidence that Paleoindians and Pleistocene animals lived side by side. In 1968 scuba diver Don Serbousek began an underwater exploration of the Aucilla (awe-SIL-a) River. On a piece of the river that now manages to stay above ground Serbousek found tools, the bones of extinct animals, some showing signs of butchering, projectile points, and chipped stones. Serbousek inferred from this find that this area during the Pleistocene era had been a deep ravine with a watering hole, a perfect spot for Paleo-man to live. Here Paleo-man would have water and access to animals coming to drink at the watering hole.

At archeological sites found underwater many items are being discovered that would have rotted away or disappeared above water. There have been excavations revealing seeds and rinds of wild gourds, a plant that was thought not to exist in Florida at this time. One underwater excavation discovered mammoth tusks, an animal hunted by the Paleoindians. When these tusks were analyzed it was shown that their growth rings showed they were migrating according to seasonal changes. It is possible that the Paleoindians followed them on their migrations staying with the herds in Florida in the warmer winters and following the herds north when summer approached. The first Florida "snowbirds."

The Florida Paleoindians probably hunted every animal they could. They made use of everything at their disposal. The animals provided food, clothing, and ligaments for bows, and bones, teeth and claws for tools. Underwater excavations have shown that the Paleoindians hunted both modern species, and species that became extinct at the end of the Pleistocene period. The supposition is that some of these Pleistocene species' became extinct due to over hunting by the Paleoindians. Case in point the Pleistocene horse. This species flourished before the Paleoindians yet after man's arrival became extinct. This does not appear to be due to climatic changes, since in the 1500s the Europeans reintroduced the horse to Florida, and these horses survived.

The Paleoindian period in Florida lasted two to three thousand years. Then the climate of Florida began to change. The Great Ice Age was loosening its grip on the world, polar ice caps began to melt, and the world grew warmer. Florida changed to a more tropical climate, and the flora and fauna changed accordingly. The Paleoindians would adjust accordingly.

CHAPTER TWO
The Archaic Period

About 8,000 years ago Florida's climate began to change. The glaciers began to melt, the climate warmed, and there was more rainfall. Sea level began to rise. The Great Ice Age was waning. Now water sources were not in such short supply, and people had more options on where they could live. Human populations increased, and the Paleoindians could begin to settle and create the start of culture.

At this time, some of the Pleistocene animals the Paleoindians relied upon for food began to decrease in numbers, some becoming extinct. Over 40 genera of animals vanished in a very short time. The Paleoindian hunters now had to hunt smaller game. Plants were also an important part of the late Pleistocene diet. Life was not easy for these Early Archaic period people. They had to hunt or gather everything they ate. They had to fashion all their containers, clothing, and other necessities. Water, though more abundant than in earlier Pleistocene times, still was scarce and highly valued.

By about 3000 BCE (Middle Archaic Period) Florida became even warmer and wetter. Sea level rose and Florida's land size shrank. The world was warming up. Native populations increased, their nascent cultures adapted to this change in climate. Populations were living in large numbers along the coasts of Florida. They moved to the St. John's river valley, where fresh water marshes provided abundant food. Small camps became villages. Cultural traditions began, such as a more sedentary lifestyle with complex social structures, and increased bureaucracy. The locations these peoples inhabited would continue to attract populations for thousands of years. Villages would be inhabited for generations.

From the villages people would travel out on hunting and gathering expeditions. Or they would gather raw materials for tool making such as chert. Chert is a flint like stone that forms in Florida's limestone outcroppings. It can be easily formed into a variety of tools—projectile points and chopping stones. For use on these forays the people would establish special use camps. These were camps where they could stay when away from their main village, akin to an early travel lodge.

By 2000 BCE (4,000 years ago, the Late Archaic Period) the populations of Florida began making fired pottery. They would put plant fibers in the clay before firing so as to strengthen the container. (In later times quartz sand, imported from the north, would be added to the clay before firing.) Prior to this time they would have used containers made from gourds, shells, basketry, or even stone. This invention of firing clay would allow new ways of preparing and storing food. This was a great technological innovation.

The successful and productive patterns of life practiced by the people of the Late Archaic Period would continue for some three thousand years. In the Late Archaic Period people were living in villages and building large construction projects. One of their most notable constructions projects were those of mound building.

Mound building is one of the most prominent features of Florida's original populations. On the coasts and along rivers, mounds built entirely of shell can be found. These mounds represent the discards of thousands of shellfish meals. Mounds found along rivers could contain shells from snails and mussels. Mounds found along the coasts could contain oyster shells and other marine life remains.

The building of these mounds was not just for the sake of disposing of inedible shells; it was an answer to the needs of these people, living in a flat Florida geography. Elevations where populations flourished would be somewhere between 50 to 100 feet above sea level or even lower. By building these mounds, and living on top of them, it offered these people a way to live above tidal and river flooding, allowed rapid rainwater disbursement, and gave them access to cooler breezes. They would contour the tops of these structures to provide flat living space. Some cultures interred their dead and used these mounds for ceremonial purposes. In areas that were not conducive to the building of shell mounds, sand mounds would be built.

The oldest known mound burial is located on Horr's Island. This island is located on Florida's southwest coast, just south of Marco Island. On Horr's Island four mounds were found. Two mounds were merely places for refuse, but two were definitely ceremonial. The largest ceremonial mound began as a huge shell pile placed on the ground. The labor to construct this mound was extensive. Carbon dating puts the construction of this mound beginning 4,000 years ago. It is estimated it took over a 1,000 years to complete the project. This mound extended nearly 20 feet above the ground surface and 40 feet above sea level.

Inside this largest mound it was found that several layers of sand had been deliberately placed. This was clean sand dug from beaches or sandbars. In one layer the sand was colored by the addition of charcoal, and basket loads of different colored sands. Two human skeletons were found buried in this mound. These graves had been dug into the mound after it was completed. Carbon 14 dating puts the date of one of the burials at 3,400 years ago, the oldest known mound burial in the eastern US.

As time went on the natives of Florida became more and more settled, engaging in more and more extensive construction and mound building projects. Their communities became more complex, politically and culturally. The introduction of agriculture to these Florida natives would bring even more complexity and stability to their lives.

About 750 AD the cultivation of corn was added to the economics of Florida. The peoples of the eastern panhandle, the Fort Walton culture, would be Florida's best farmers. Living between the Aucilla and Apalachicola rivers, these peoples engaged in intensive agricultural pursuits. Some of the Fort Walton peoples were the ancestors of the

Apalachee, one of the cultures encountered by the first Europeans explorers. As with other native farmers in the Southeast, Fort Walton farmers grew a major portion of their diet. Growing not only corn, but also beans, squash, pumpkins, and sunflowers.

With the introduction of agriculture came increases in populations, increased bureaucracy, and the beginning of trade. Floridians became part of an elaborate trade network extending from the Great Lakes to the Gulf of Mexico, and extending west to Oklahoma.

Because Florida is surrounded by water, it provided its people with commodities highly valued in more northerly, inland areas. The coastal peoples of Florida could gather shells that made wonderful dippers, bowls, and tools. Shells could be polished and made into beads and necklaces. Some shells were so exquisite they were prized for their beauty alone. In the shallow coastal waters sharks' teeth could be harvested. These shark teeth were useful in all sorts of tools. All of these items were bartered, and they can be traced up the North American continent. Gulf coast shells have been found as far west as Oklahoma, and as far north as Wisconsin. In archeological finds in Kentucky it has been discovered people living in the area 5,000 years ago were wearing beads made from marine shells and drinking from vessels made of whelk shells, a shell found in Florida. In archeological finds in Florida dated 5,000 years ago we find pots and throwing stick weights made of soapstone quarried in Georgia.

In the Late Archaic Period, with the development of pottery, trade expanded. Fiber tempered pots from Florida have been found at Poverty Point Site in northwest Louisiana. From Poverty Point goods were shipped north throughout the southeastern US. In Florida beads and figures carved from Poverty Point red jasper were worn as adornment.

It is likely Florida seafood that was dried or smoked was traded. Sharkskin, tortoise shell, and plant products were traded. Cassina (ka SEEN a), the leaves of which make up the caffeine-rich "black drink," used in purification rituals was highly valued in the north, since the cassina plant (*ilex vomitoria*) only grows in warmer climates. To salt-starved inland peoples, salt from seawater would have been an important trade element.

Floridians wanted from their northern neighbors copper breastplates used in ritual, high-grade chert for tools, and scapstone. As agriculture intensified in Florida and social and religious ritual became more complex, the demand increased for more and more elaborate and exotic items from the north. Priests and chieftains ruling these agricultural bureaucracies required elaborate objects that symbolized their power and religion. The distribution of these ritual oriented objects was widespread. Even small villages would have a few of these symbolic objects. Showing how pervasive trade was among these early Floridians. Florida's natives were living well. Their land and cultures were rich and varied. But, there was a force heading their way that most of them would not survive. Soon they would face their biggest challenges ever.

CHAPTER THREE
The Europeans

The first European to come to southern shores was of course Christopher Columbus. He actually landed on the island of Hispaniola (now the Dominican Republic and Haiti.) He was not out to find a new land what he wanted to find was Cathy (China) with its wealth of spices and silks. What Columbus did though was open up a New World to a myriad of explorers all looking for wealth for themselves and the rulers of the countries they sailed for. Some explorers were embarking on a religious mission—converting the natives to Christianity.

When Columbus returned with the stories of his trip, explorers such as Cortes, Pizarro, and Ponce de Leon all began to dream of riches in this new land. Cortes was to find enormous wealth in Mexico in his conquest and massacre of the Aztecs, and Pizarro found even greater wealth in South America with his conquest and massacre of the Incas. Ponce de Leon wanted a piece of this action.

During the 16th century Spain's economy relied on the wealth coming from the New World. This actually was unfortunate because this great influx of gold lead to the downfall of the Spanish economy. These easy riches created inflation, higher taxes, and the loss of peasant labor. Peasants could no longer afford to live in Spain so they left for the New World. Spain, at this time, also was fighting an expensive war with France, this war funded with the gold coming into the country from the New World. Spain was desperate to keep its strong position in Europe that meant it needed more gold from the New World. The Spanish monarchy was most willing to fund exploration of these new lands in search of the riches they held.

Juan Ponce de Leon was related to Spanish kings, in fact, he was a page in the royal court of Spain when he set out to find wealth in the New World. On the island of Puerto Rico Ponce de Leon did find gold. He conquered the island and became its governor. But he wanted more. He had heard tales from the natives that north of Puerto Rico lay a land that held a magical spring that would give one eternal youth. Of course he never found the spring.

When Juan Ponce de Leon arrived in La Florida in 1513 there were hundreds of different native societies living in every part of the state. The lives of these native peoples would soon be threatened. Florida drew colonists from Spain, France, and Great Britain. Conquistadors, entrepreneurs, soldiers, missionaries, and settlers all came to Florida seeking their futures.

Over a decade before Ponce de Leon's voyage, John Cabot, sailing for England, had sailed southward along the Atlantic coast to an unknown southerly point. Cabot's and Ponce de Leon's voyage along with other adventurers' voyages, led to fierce competition for the land called Florida. Unfortunately for the Florida Indians, they ended up caught in these international conflicts, and did not survive them.

When Ponce de Leon first sighted Florida he needed firewood and fresh water. Anxious to see what this new land was like, he sent some men ashore. Skirmishes took place with the Indians and two Spaniards were wounded. One Indian was kidnapped, the Spanish wanting him to be a guide. The first Indian and European encounters were not friendly. Ponce de Leon was out to enslave the natives. It was said he was bloodthirsty and cruel. He wanted to find gold at all costs. Ponce de Leon sailed south to Biscayne Bay, where he found the Tequesta (ta KES ta) Indians, a tribe living at the mouth of the Miami River. He continued on around the Keys and turned north toward Calusa territory, a tribe living in southwest Florida.

There were more skirmishes with the Calusas. The Calusas would canoe or catamaran out to the Spaniards' ships and attack them with bows and arrows. There were fatalities on both sides, yet each wanted to know the other better. Each side wanted to establish trade.

In 1521 Ponce de Leon returned to Florida for a second time. He was intent on starting a colony. He most probably landed in Calusa territory. He came with 200 men, Catholic clergy, seeds for crop planting, and livestock. Ponce de Leon was not a successful colonizer, in fact he received a poisoned arrow injury in an Indian and European encounter. He finally left for Cuba, where he died from an infection from the arrow's wound. The 1520s found the Gulf of Mexico ruled by Spain, and the entire coastline from southern Florida to the Yucatan had been mapped, including Tampa Bay and Charlotte Harbor. (Though cartography was not yet an exact science.)

The Spanish were sure they could successfully occupy La Florida. In 1526 the crown had contracted seasoned conquistador Panfilo de Narvaez to colonize the lands between the northern Gulf coast of Mexico and northwest Florida. This would give Spain a land bridge from Mexico to the Atlantic Coast. Unfortunately for Narvaez due to poor cartography, he landed in Tampa Bay. Thinking it was Charlotte Harbor, 90 miles south of Tampa, Narvaez marched his men northward to find the supposed Tampa Bay. He of course never found this more northern harbor and his expedition disintegrated.

By August 1537, the sole Narvaez survivor returned to Spain and told people of his adventures in La Florida. It was thought La Florida was the richest land in the world. These stories enticed another conquistador to explore La Florida-Hernando de Soto.

At first De Soto sailed for Cuba, where he claimed his title as governor. In Cuba De Soto set up base for his exploration of Florida. In May 1539, an expedition of five large and four smaller ships sailed. In seven days the fleet anchored off of Longboat Key. Over the next several days they moved to Tampa Bay. De Soto set up camp along the Little Manatee River. There were 750 people, 220 horses, pigs, and supplies offloaded at that camp. By 1543 only 310 people, all in rags, would leave Florida, leaving behind all they had brought, and De Soto as well.

During his expedition in Florida De Soto had planned to live off the stored foods of the Indians. He would use native guides to lead him to large villages and stockpiles of stored food. It was a good plan, but it didn't work. De Soto's native guides deliberately lead him away from the larger villages and the stockpiles of food. Many times villagers knowing of De Soto's treachery towards the Indians would abandon their homes and take their food stores with them when they knew he was heading their way.

De Soto not finding the wealth he wanted in Florida, marched into Georgia and South Carolina, and finally came into Tennessee. He finally headed back to Alabama, and to Mississippi. He went to Arkansas and crossed the Mississippi River. In 1541 he returned to the camp he had made on the Mississippi, De Soto took ill and died in June of 1541. Fifteen years later the Spanish tried another attempt to colonize Florida, but failed again.

In 1562 France was well aware of Spain's attempt to colonize Florida, in that year France would send its own expedition to La Florida. This first expedition was prompted by France's attempts to look for gold in the New World. France was very jealous of Spain's success. Led by Jean Ribaut (ree-BOW), the 150-person expedition landed near St. Augustine. Ribaut was a devoted Protestant. Protestants at this time were being persecuted in France. He felt by colonizing Florida he could establish a home for the Protestants, show France Protestant loyalty, and find gold and land for France. He sailed north to the mouth of the St. Johns River and claimed this area for France. This news reached Spain, and plans to counter this French aggression were being considered. France now had a tenuous hold on Florida. There was a second French expedition in 1564. This second expedition claimed more land for France establishing Fort Caroline (near today's city of Jacksonville.)

But La Florida would not remain in French hands. Spain sent Pedro Menendez de Aviles in 1565 to oust France and establish a Spanish colony. Menendez had the vision of Florida as a great Spanish colony with an economy based on pearl fishing, agriculture, and mining. Menendez operating out of St. Augustine managed to remove the French presence. He and his men marched to Fort Caroline. For three days they trudged north, through snake and mosquito infested swamps.

The French thought they were safe in their fort. This was hurricane season and the rains were constant. The French couldn't believe anyone would attack in such horrible weather. No one was on guard at Fort Caroline. The battle didn't last an hour. When the battle was over most of the French soldiers were dead. Those that surrendered were killed. A few made it back to France where they told of the horrible massacre.

The Spanish built San Mateo where Fort Caroline had been. They also built forts along the coast up to South Carolina. The French still angry over the destruction of Fort Caroline sent a revenge mission to San Mateo, destroying it. Yet this would not be enough to keep Florida French. Florida would be a Spanish colony for the next two hundred years.

In an effort to stabilize this colony for Spain, it was decided to erect Spanish missions and build garrisons. Pedro Menendez de Aviles in 1565 was enlisted to secure the Florida coasts and assure Spain's access to its sea-lanes. Jesuits were brought in to staff missions; and garrisons would be built at the mouths of Florida rivers. The proposed garrisons would be at Tampa Bay among the Tocobaga (to KO ba ga) Indians, the Caloosahatchee River among the Calusas, the Miami River among the Tequesta, and the mouth of the St. Johns River among the Timucua. One of the mandates of Menendez's plan was to convert the native populations to Catholicism. By doing so and training the Indians in the ways of the Spanish he would be assured loyalty to Spain. Unfortunately none of this worked out for Menendez.

Coastal garrisons and missions were established, but only lasted a few years. By 1572 the Jesuits withdrew from Florida. In 1573 the Franciscans came to Florida and sowed the seeds of Catholicism, and the ultimate demise of most of the Florida Indians.

In 1586 English sea captain Francis Drake burned and plundered St. Augustine. St. Augustine survived becoming the oldest European settlement in North America. For the next 100 years and more, France, England, and Spain argued and fought over whom had the right to this land called Florida. Florida's natives had no say in the matter.

Florida's Indians would not survive the events between 1565 and 1763. Between epidemics, and military conflicts between international powers-Great Britain, France, and Spain, the native peoples of Florida did not stand a chance. By the 1760s the human legacy of 10-12,000 years would vanish. The native population of Florida in 1513, when Ponce de Leon came to Florida was estimated to be anywhere from 100,000 to 350,000 people. By the 1760s warfare, slave raiding, and epidemics of disease left only 1,000 native people alive!

This population vacuum attracted Native Americans that sought a different kind of wealth...land and the possibility of living in peace. These Native Americans that moved into Florida in the early part of the eighteenth century were Lower Creeks from Georgia and Alabama. In 1767 a band of upper Creeks settled around Tampa Bay.

Spain, owner of La Florida, at this time, encouraged this movement of Creeks into the area. With the demise of so much of the native population, Spain needed to rebuild its population base. Florida presented new opportunities for the Creeks, and they happily took advantage of them.

Originally the Creeks that moved into Florida retained much of their original culture. But gradually they began to develop a new way of life, more attuned to their new surroundings. These native peoples also received a new name-Seminole. This name coming from *yat'siminoli*, meaning "free people." The name denoting foreigners had never dominated them. English speakers ignored the fact there were other tribes living in Florida, and called all Florida tribes Seminoles. The Seminoles brought with them two languages-the Mikasuki (mik AH suk e) (Hitchiti) language, of the Lower Creeks, and the Muskogee (mus KO ge) language of the Upper Creeks. Florida offered this new population a fertile land with good hunting; chances to create new cultural ways; and distance from the Indian and international intrigues that were occurring in Georgia and Alabama.

CHAPTER FOUR

The Seminoles Arrive

Important aspects of Creek life were maintained by the native population moving into Florida, including ceremonies such as the smoking of the peace pipe, taking the "black drink," (a herbal emetic) for purification rites, and celebration of the Green Corn Dance. The Green Corn Dance's ritual base revolving around maintaining the balance of world purity, creating a balance of nature, and promoting agricultural fertility. All these activities and beliefs have a long history among the native peoples of the Southeast, including the ancestors of the Seminoles.

In their new homeland there were opportunities to acquire wealth through trading and bartering; this made entrepreneurs of many of the Seminoles. Men and women acquired status and power from these entrepreneurial accomplishments. Individuals and their families, not just town councils, began to emerge as economic decision-makers. This was a great change from the static and hereditary bureaucracy they left in the Creek Confederation to the north of Florida. The Seminoles were now able to create their own governments based on fairness. No longer did they have to deal with the political intrigues of the Creeks.

Each village and tribe had a civil government headed by a chief. The chief would make decisions on food storage, feasts, public works, and community agricultural projects. A council of advisors would assist the chief. There were women town leaders as well as men. The leaders would be selected on the basis of competence and experience. Always on issues of great importance the chief and counsel would seek the general consensus of all the people. Each village also had a head war chief. He would be in charge of overseeing military decisions. This chief was always a proven warrior. A person others would follow.

If there was a conflict and war was declared each member of the war party was responsible for his own weapons, and his own provisions. The entire war party also had to be acceptable to the supernatural world. Before setting out, there were purification ceremonies such as fasting, sweating, bathing and the taking of the "black drink." When returning from war, warriors were considered polluted and had to go through purification rites again so as not to upset the supernatural world.

As with other southeastern native societies, the Seminoles were matri- lineal-children belonged to the same clan as their mothers. When a man married he had to marry outside of his clan. Clans were important eco- nomic units, both for the production of food and goods for trade. A clan was responsible for the welfare of its members. A boy did not belong to his father's clan, so, one of his mother's brothers (uncles on his mother's side), or perhaps one of her cousins, if she did not have brothers, would instruct the boy in hunting, fishing, and the rituals of war. Girls, since they were members of their mother's clan, would be given guidance from their mother.

When a man married he would move into the household of his bride. There he would live among women who may span several generations, all of the same clan. There might be a great-grandmother, a grandmother, her daughters, and the adult daughter's unmarried children, and married daughters. The oldest female in the household would have the final say on household matters. Women were the teachers of Seminole ways. It was this tradition that gave the Seminoles strength during their trials and tribulations with the white man.

If all the females of a clan were to die the clan would die as well. This has happened, there once was an alligator clan, but when the last female of that clan died the clan died with her. There are currently eight clans of the Florida Seminoles-Panther, Bear, Deer, Wind, Big Town, Bird, Snake, and Otter.

The father of the children was responsible for the support of his children and almost always had a warm relationship with them, yet his children did not belong to his clan. Thus, every man's first responsibility was to the children of his sister, since they were of the same clan as he.

Because a marriage created an alliance between clans, there was much consideration given to the union. Older clan kin arranged marriages. The elders of a young man's clan would discuss the possible marriage with the elders of the young woman's clan. Even after preliminary arrangements were made for the marriage, still the couple had to give their consent. No one was forced to marry.

If the elders and the couple agreed to the marriage, then the young man would give gifts to the bride-to-be's relatives. This to repay them for their loss of her help in the household. Also, this showed the maturity and responsibility of the young man. Once the gifts were accepted, the couple could begin to live together, though usually there was a celebration—a feast, in honor of the marriage.

If a man was a very good hunter, and could provide more food and hides than one woman could manage, he could take another wife. He could only do this with the consent of the first wife; she remained the principal wife. The first wife usually was happy to have the extra help. Also, the fact that she was married to a man that could keep more than one wife gave her social status. The man would build separate housing for each wife to keep household harmony.

Because of the matrilineal system, personal property of the household belonged to the woman. If she decided to divorce, the man would have to move back to his mother's house and his former wife kept the household belongings, and the children. The father would still see his children and be responsible for supporting them.

Disciplining of children rested on the mother or the mother's brothers. Seminole children, it was noted by white settlers, were very obedient, even though usually the only punishment given was that of scratching the skin with a sharp object. This form of punishment was more humiliating than painful. A visible scratch mark meant the person had misbehaved. The transgressor was shamed before all of society. A similar ritual was performed in purification rites. The Seminoles considered blood letting as a way to let the evil out of an individual.

Among the Seminole, the tasks of gathering and growing were "women's work." The men helped when there was intensive work to do, such as clearing land and harvesting. The men's primary tasks were hunting, fishing, and warfare. Europeans noted that it appeared the men were lazy, the women doing all the work. But, the men's tasks though not as continuous as the women's still were demanding.

Animals were hunted for both their meat and their hides. Deer was the most valuable, since the meat was prime, and they had a large smooth hide which was tanned by the women, and used as clothing. The men also hunted squirrels, raccoons, and bear. Bear was especially prized for its furry hide and its fat. The fat was used for cooking, and for dressing of the hair and oiling of the skin. Turkeys, ducks, and geese were popular foods as well. Turtles, shellfish, fresh and saltwater fish were hunted as well as alligators. Food was plentiful and varied for these early Seminoles. They truly had come to a land of plenty.

In hunting large game the men used guns, bows and arrows, spears, and knives. Each hunter made his own bows, arrows, and spears; guns and knives were traded for with the outside world. Young boys would learn by first imitating the weapons of older men, using these "weapons" in play. Then later they would study under the guidance of an older male. Many times the men hunted as a team. They would bait deer with corn hidden in the myrtles and then two hunters would appear to assure a sure shot. Or, they would wear deerskins, complete with heads and antlers and thus approach a herd of deer without frightening them.

For catching fish, men used hooks and lines, nets, and gorges—sharp pieces of wood or bone tied to a line. These would become lodged in the fish's throat, immobilizing the fish. In some areas, a poison was used to immobilize the fish. The fish could literally be lifted from the water.

Women were responsible for preparing and cooking the food. They baked, boiled, or broiled it, often adding vegetables to boiled meat to create a stew. The women thickened the stew with cornmeal. Fruits and some vegetables were dried to preserve them. Tubers and roots were boiled, baked, or pounded into flour.

The most important aspect to the Seminole diet was corn (maize.) The Seminoles grew corn (maize), beans, and squash on raised areas of land called "hammocks." These agricultural crops gave variety to their diet as well as creating a basis for a stable agricultural society. The drink of the Seminoles—Sofkee (sof KEY) was made from corn. Women would roast the ears of corn to separate the corn from the cob, pound the kernels, and then boil them into a liquid consistency. Cornmeal was made from dried corn that was soaked and softened, and pounded into a fine meal. A batter of cornmeal and water was wrapped in cornhusks and boiled to make a form of bread. The men would take this bread when they went on hunting or warring expeditions.

Hominy was the favorite dish of the Seminoles. Mixing corn kernels with wood ashes and soaking the mixture overnight started the process. This loosened the outer covering of the kernels. The women then pounded the corn to remove the hulls and cooked the kernels in water for several hours. The result was thinned with water, mashed, and made into a drink or made into a stew.

The Seminoles would walk to nearby destinations, but for traversing any long distances, people and their possessions traveled by dugout canoe. Dugouts would mainly be made from the trunk of the bald cypress tree. These trees were large enough, buoyant enough, easy to work, and always grew close to the water. This meant the tree trunk would not have to be transported any long distance during the making of the dugout, or after its completion.

When the men found a suitable tree, they would start by burning the base they then would fell it by chipping it with axes. The cypress would then be carried to a clearing, and placed in a horizontal position. The men would build a fire on the tree, and carefully control how much of the tree would be burnt. They would scrape away the burnt wood, and gradually carve out the log. The outside of the canoe would be shaped with axes and adzes. These dugouts would then be propelled by paddle, pole, or sail. It has been reported the Seminoles could travel all the way to Cuba in these vessels.

Housing for the Seminoles, since the mid-nineteenth century, was the traditional grouping of chikkees (CHICK keys.) This distinctive shelter is composed of cypress poles and a thatched palmetto roof. Chikkees have raised platforms for sitting and sleeping, and most are open sided. These structures are perfectly adapted to the climate of south Florida. They afford protection from the sun and rain, and allow maximum exposure to breezes. They also were easy to assemble and disassemble in case of hurricane, high water, or if the white man were chasing them and the Seminoles needed to break camp quickly.

Chikkees were traditionally built in clusters. Each chikkee serving as a room, not a whole house. The total number of chikkees would change to accommodate the members of the extended family. A typical family camp would include at least four chikkees. Each would be of a different design, depending on its use. A cooking chikkee would be the center structure; around it would be dining, utility, and sleeping chikkees. Each family's group of chikkees would encircle the main council house in the village creating a sense of community for all.

Several generations of women would gather under the shelter of their chickee to sew, talk, teach, and prepare their meal. Women tended the fire in their cooking chickee. The cooking chickee was a central symbol of hearth and home for the Seminoles. A woman's place was by the fire. It was up to her the control her own life and carry out the cooking. When a woman grew old it was up to her to have a home and have a fire going.

Palm logs would be used to fuel the cooking fire. The logs emanating from the fire's center like the spokes of a giant rimless wheel. One of the women would adjust the logs to control the fire under the cooking pot.

There were usually four logs used for a fire, they represented the Four Corners of the earth. Each Seminole clan had their own interpretation of the meaning of each of the four logs, and how to take care of their camp. The Seminoles believed that "medicine or singing" could protect the fire. Many times an animal spirit would be summoned to protect the flames. The same "medicine" could be used to keep the family together.

Seminoles believed they lived in an orderly society where nature was balanced. Yet this balance could easily be upset. When they hunted they realized they upset nature, thus they would apologize to the animals and go through ritual purification after hunting. If these rituals were not followed, nature would be angry and send disease and discomfort. Sickness and death were explained as the result of broken rules or impurity. It is hard to imagine what the Seminoles thought when European diseases plagued them. They must have suffered miserably not only physically but mentally as well. They must have desperately tried to restore the natural balance. Little did they know it was to no avail.

Shamans—sometimes called "medicine men or women" would be called in to set the universe right again. To do this the shaman would have to determine if anyone was polluted or had committed a taboo. If it were determined that someone was polluted, that person would have to purify him or herself, sometimes by fasting. Fasting meant one would first clean out their stomach with a drink made from herbs—the "black drink." This drink cleared the stomach of its contents, and then the fast could begin. Once purified the person returned to balance with nature, and was now fit to carry out their usual activities. As long as they lived within the laws of nature, all would be well.

The annual Green Corn Dance (busk ceremonies) celebrated the Seminoles sacred bond with their environment. The land sustained them, without it their way of life would perish. Each year sometime between April to early July, the date determined by the head shaman, the Corn Dance rituals were performed. This ceremony was vital to the continuation of Seminole culture. The event was a great pleasure to the people, and necessary to hold them together as a society. There was dancing, feasting, and a general good time at the Green Corn Dance.

During this four to seven day period, the symbolic objects given by the Great Spirit to the Seminoles were displayed. This was the only time of the year that they were shown. These objects allowed the Seminoles to carry on their collective life. The Great Spirit would send emissaries with additional objects as conditions changed. The total of old and new objects were kept together. This "medicine bundle" contained all the medicine they needed to protect and preserve their way of life, as long as the medicine was handled with proper ritual.

On one of the days of the ceremony there would be Court Day. On this day the elders would judge the most serious infractions of tribal mores. Also men, who had earned the right, could dispense with their baby names and receive a more honorable title.

Women did not participate in the first stages of the ceremony. Men and older boys would purify themselves by fasting, and drinking the "black drink." All males were scratched to cleanse themselves. While the men were fasting the women cleaned their homes and extinguished the fire in their fire pits, and the head shaman extinguished the fire that constantly burned in the council house. This symbolized the casting out of the old and impure. The head shaman of the village would then solemnly rekindle the fire in the council house, a symbol of rebirth. The women would then take coals from this main fire to start new fires in their fire pits.

After the lighting of the new fires, a great feast was prepared from the new crops. Everyone shared in this feast, danced, and played games. It was a joyous occasion. Even couples, who had eloped, to avoid arranged marriages, could return at this time and be forgiven. Then their elopement would be an accepted marriage, and they were allowed to live in the village again. The Green Corn Dance kept the world in order, maintained balance, and cast out the old and impure, and eliminated spiritual pollution.

The Seminoles, for the first hundred years of their stay in Florida, enjoyed the richness of this great land, their new cultural heritage, and their freedom and citizenship under Spanish rule. As with the other four main tribes in the South (Choctaw, Chickasaw, Cherokee, and Creek) the Seminoles would be in the way of American expansionism and a growing US army. Americans were a people that felt powerful and wanted more, whether this meant land, money, or slaves. The Indians had to be dealt with.

CHAPTER FIVE
A Recipe For War

The year is 1811...

"For a hundred summers our warriors have reposed undisturbed under the shade of their live oaks. The suns of one hundred winters have risen on our ardent pursuit of the buck and the bear, with no dispute to our bounds or range of territory." (Spoken by Seminole representatives.) Of course, white settlers had a different opinion.

The Native American wars of the South and East have been minimized—rather the emphasis has been on the conflicts with the indigenous peoples of the Plains. Yet the three wars of the Seminoles are some of the most dramatic episodes in history. During the Seminole Wars the Indians defended their homes in Florida at an appalling human cost. They defied the efforts of the white people to dislodge them from their country. They clung tenaciously to their liberty and land. By their courage and expert strategy they exposed to ridicule an invading army nearly ten times their number. The Seminoles were hunted like animals, their homes and villages destroyed. They were driven into almost inaccessible swamps with only their resourcefulness to sustain them. On top of all this most were carried off as prisoners to an inhospitable place called Indian Territory.

The Seminoles concerned white settlers for two main reasons—one, they were pro Spanish, and two they harbored runaway slaves from Southern United States plantations. It was well known to plantation slaves, if they could make it to Spanish Florida they would escape the yoke of plantation bondage. The fact the Seminoles harbored these "runaways" would become a major issue leading to the Seminole Wars and Indian relocation to the West. Whites could not tolerate the fact that the Seminoles had "their property."

The Seminoles did keep some of these "runaways" as "slaves." Unlike plantation bondage though the Seminole "slaves" were allowed to establish their own villages, carry guns, acquire livestock, practice agriculture, and build homes for themselves. For this the Seminoles asked for a reasonable portion of their harvest. It was a mutually beneficial situation—the Seminoles would provide protection for the blacks, and the blacks paid a modest amount in return. Seminole "slavery" was more akin to European feudalism.

Another advantage, to the Seminoles, of having a black population was that most blacks spoke some form of European language—English or Spanish. The blacks soon learned their patrons' Muskegon dialect and the blacks knew the ways of the Europeans. Thus, these "runaways" became valuable to the Seminoles as interpreters, and even counselors.

In the early 1800s there was a trail of international intrigue entangling the blacks and tribesmen of Florida. Florida was still owned by Spain, but the United States looked longingly at settling this rich new land. On January 15, 1811, Congress allowed President Madison and "local authorities" to seize any or all of Florida. In March of 1812, so-called "Patriots," hoisted the United States flag on Amelia Island, a site northeast of Jacksonville. Then some 400 Patriots moved south. The Spanish were too weak to resist them. Spain's only hopes of resistance were the Seminoles and their blacks. The Patriots had no respect for the Seminoles, and began dividing up their land among themselves. The Seminoles faced losing their homes to these land-hungry Americans, and the blacks faced a return to plantation slavery. The Americans feared the blacks of Florida would encourage American slaves to revolt. In June 1812, a group of Tennesseans prepared to march under General Andrew Jackson against British-held Mobile and Spanish held Pensacola. Eastern Tennesseans had organized a regiment of volunteer cavalry. The Seminoles sued for peace through Creek Indian agent Benjamin Hawkins. But the Americans proceeded.

Many Seminoles retreated to the woods. The soldiers began to plunder and sack their villages. They killed 50 to 60 tribesmen, and destroyed the Seminole food supply. The eastern Florida peninsula was now open to settlers.

A joint force of Seminoles and blacks struck plantations along the St. Johns River in July of 1812. Escaped slaves from Georgia joined in fighting the American settlers. Some joined the Seminoles some joined Spanish forces. The Spanish governor proclaimed, "Freedom to every Negro who fought for Spain."

Tribal and black resistance allowed opponents to the annexation of Florida to prevail in Congress. The Patriot movement fell apart, and the group accepted peace terms from Spain in 1816. This then ended, temporarily; the US attempt to seize Spanish owned East Florida. An uneasy peace prevailed, the Seminoles and their blacks on one side and the full force of the American army on the other.

CHAPTER SIX

The First Seminole War

In the early 1800's another large migration of Creeks came into Florida. Some 1,000 Upper Creeks came following Andrew Jackson's defeat of the Upper Creeks at the Battle of Tohopeka (to ho PEE ka.) This battle was part of a Creek civil war, this Creek civil war largely due to the influence of Creek Indian Agent Benjamin Hawkins. Hawkins had sought to break down the communal ways of the Creeks. He wanted to have all the Creeks look to the white man's capitalistic ways. In this way Hawkins hoped he would solidify the Creek Confederation so that he would have one responsible counterpart to deal with. Ironically this worked exactly the opposite. Some Creeks adopted the white man's capitalistic outlook some stayed with the Creek communal ways. This cleavage was too much for the Creeks to deal with and war broke out among them. Andrew Jackson, interceding in this war was a way to deal a blow to the native populations and free lands for settlers from the expanding United States. Jackson sided with one group of Upper Creeks against the Upper Creeks known as "Red Sticks." They were a division of the Creeks whose custom was to declare war by erecting a red pole in the center of the village. The "Red Sticks" would migrate to Florida and carry their communal ways with them.

Jackson, in The Treaty of Fort Jackson, 1815, had Creek chiefs loyal to the United States, cede 22 million acres of what had been Creek land in Georgia and Alabama to the United States. The "Red Sticks" would never forget what the Creeks loyal to the US had done. The Creeks loyal to the US were given land in Southeast Alabama, though this land was held in trust by the US government.

During the war of 1812 the British regarded the Indians of the Gulf Coast potential allies. One of the things they did to cement this relationship was to build a fort at Prospect Bluff, fifteen miles above the mouth of the Apalachicola River, and sixty miles south of US territory. They equipped this fort with cannon, arms, and a large store of ammunition. When the British left after their defeat in the 1812 war, the fort was left intact for the Indians. This fort though came under the control of a band of free renegade blacks. By 1816 it was an effective stronghold. It was called the Negro Fort.

Feeling victorious from his dealings in the north, and seeking an easier way to service US forts north of Florida, in 1816 General Andrew Jackson invaded Spanish Florida and attacked Seminole towns. Jackson advanced against the fort on the Apalachicola River. The Negro Fort stood in the way of his supplying US forts from the easy access of the Gulf of Mexico.

Jackson fired on the fort from the river, lucky for Jackson, the fort was destroyed when a red-hot cannon ball, hit the powder magazine. This explosion killed or wounded all 300 blacks in the fort. Stunned by this catastrophe, Seminoles and blacks remained quiet for several months. Blacks found refuge along the Suwanee River, and began reorganizing. They built villages, near the Seminoles. The Seminoles planned retaliatory raids against Americans on the Georgia border.

Early in 1817 it was claimed six hundred armed blacks were marching to drumbeats. The same number of tribesmen accompanied the blacks. The blacks agreed to serve with the Seminole warriors, but in their own companies, and under their own captains. They swore revenge for the destruction of Fort Negro.

The next clash came at a place called Fowl Town, a village in Georgia, near the Florida line. About 45 Mikasuki Seminole warriors and their families lived in the village. Neamathla (knee HA ma he,) chief of the village, had warned the Americans "not to cross or cut a stick of wood on the East Side of the Flint River." Neamathla was considered to be an uncommonly capable leader. He was bold, violent, and unable to submit to a superior or endure an equal. Yet in response to Neamathla's request the Americans attacked. They drove the Seminoles into the swamps and killed approximately 20 in the process. The troops plundered and burned the town.

The Seminole and black revenge for Fowl Town was swift. Across the US border slaves were seized, plantations were raided, and livestock was taken by the Seminoles. Andrew Jackson was anxious to deal with this situation and was put in command of the American troops. In April 1818, a Tennessee regiment sacked many Mikasuki and Seminole villages, and headed toward more villages along the Suwanee. The villages were warned of this. The Seminoles crossed the Suwanee and disappeared into the swamps. The blacks were not as quick to get across the river and had to face Jackson and his army. The men desperately held their ground. They fought as long as they could but finally had to retreat across the river. Jackson now possessed a deserted town, a few livestock, and some corn. Jackson and his Creek scouts tried to find the Seminoles, but they had scattered in the swamps.

May of 1818, Jackson entered Spanish held Pensacola, and forced it to surrender to him. He then left a small force behind, and headed home. Jackson was severely criticized by the American government for his seizure of Spanish Florida, but idolized by American frontiersmen. Now Florida's Seminoles and blacks were constantly moving. They were mainly heading south.

Jackson had marched mainly unopposed through Florida. His ease of action showed Spain it could not keep Florida. Although President Monroe returned Jackson's conquests to Spain in August 1818, Spain realized Florida would be lost to the Americans. In February 1819, the Adams-Onis treaty was signed by Spain, ceding Florida to the US for 5 million dollars and the release of American claims in Texas. Formal transfer of Florida occurred in 1821. Andrew Jackson was named the first Florida territorial governor, but only served for a few months.

Tired of the continuous conflicts and seeking peace, in 1823 the Seminoles signed a peace treaty at Moultrie Creek (near St. Augustine.) This treaty guaranteed the Seminoles hunting and crop grounds in the center of Florida. The Seminoles were promised equipment, livestock, and an annual payment of $5,000 for 20 years as reparation for the loss of their land in northern Florida. In return for 30 million acres of fertile farmland, they received 5 million acres of land unfit for cultivation. The Seminoles also agreed they would no longer protect escaped slaves.

It took the Seminoles more than a year to move to this reservation. They had no means to sustain themselves, and were soon afflicted by hunger. Also, non-Seminoles continued to raid Seminole villages for runaway slaves, even though this violated the Moultrie Creek treaty. The Seminoles were too exhausted from the recent war to resist. Hungry and resentful they grew more discontent. The Seminoles realized life under US rule would be less pleasant than under Spanish rule. Under Spanish rule, they had been given land and citizenship. Under US rule their land was taken, and they were not citizens.

With the rise of Jacksonian democracy in the United States in the 1820s-1830s a national program of Indian displacement was enacted, this for the benefit of white settlers and land speculators. In 1830, during the administration of Andrew Jackson, the Indian Removal Act became the law of the land. The southeastern natives were to be moved west of the Mississippi River to Indian Territory, now known as Oklahoma.

In 1832 there was a treaty signed at Payne's Landing (north central Florida.) This treaty set aside lands in Indian Territory for relocation of the Seminoles, Choctaws, Chickasaws, Cherokees, and Creeks. The Seminoles refused to leave. The Seminoles claimed they had been duped into signing this treaty. Because of their resistance to removal from their homeland these brave people incurred the wrath of the US Government. Federal militia was sent to deal with the situation; armed conflict was inevitable. The US Government could not believe a few thousand Indians would have the audacity to defy a country of 15,000,000? The stage was set for the Second Seminole War.

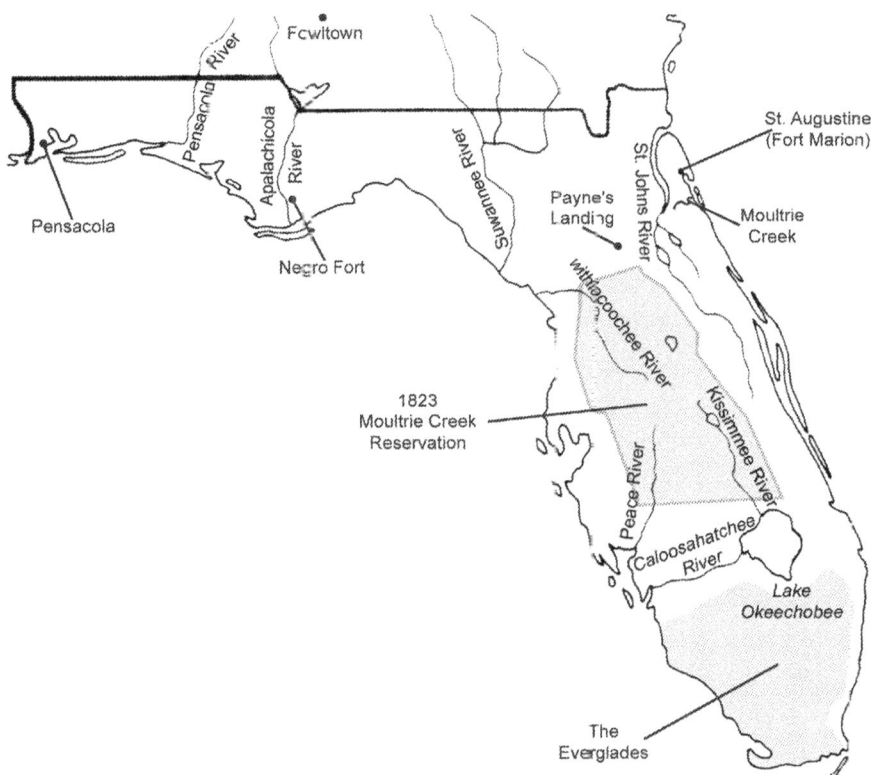

CHAPTER SEVEN
The Issue of Slavery

Slavery had been the backbone of Southern agriculture for years before the Seminole conflicts. The South was a major producer of tobacco, rice, corn, indigo, sugar, and of course "king" cotton. With the invention of the cotton gin in 1793 cotton fields were expanded since now cotton became a very profitable venture. The South produced cotton not only for the US but for the looms of England as well. Because of the vastness of these plantations, the need for human chattel as labor was imperative. Two events in history made the Southern plantation owners most concerned with the slave issue. On January 1, 1808, the Federal Government prohibited the importation of any new slaves into the US, and in August 1831, a slave, Nat Turner, led a rebellion of 70 slaves against whites in Virginia. About 57 whites were killed before this rebellion was crushed. Slave owners now faced not only a potential shortage of slaves but also possible slave rebellions as well. So when the white population expanded into Florida protection of their slave property, and fear of slave rebellion were considered serious threats.

In the early 1800s, well to do planter families from Maryland, Virginia, North and South Carolina, and Georgia began to move into Florida. They established plantations between the Apalachicola and Suwanee rivers and developed a slave-based economy. Yet in Florida, unlike other Southern states there existed a population of runaway slaves and free blacks that created alliances with the native population—the Seminoles. The planters that settled in Florida realized there were potentially troubled relations with their slaves in Florida because of these alliances. In response they enacted severe slave codes and other race-related statutes designed to ensure physical and psychological control over their property.

If a slave were to runaway, in Florida, and had no familial ties he would logically make his way to a Seminole settlement and stay. This caused great concern to the plantation slave owners. Disputes between whites and Indians over black slaves were a very prominent feature of Native American removal from Florida. The difference between Indian removal in Florida and in other areas of the United States was that land was not the main issue. There were thousands of acres of land that could be used in Florida without dispossessing the Seminoles. The problem was the issue of black slavery. When attempts to resolve these issues between whites and Seminoles were made they always failed. They failed mainly because the federal Indian agents owned and speculated in slaves, thus they suffered from a conflict of interest. The Seminoles also did not want to give up their valued interpreters, guides, and helpers—the blacks.

In the 1820s it was reported that there were some four hundred blacks living with the Seminoles, yet only 80 could truly be identified as runaway slaves. Whites that came into the area were aghast at how brazen these blacks were. According to an army surgeon Jacob Rhett Motte, "They had none of the servility of our northern blacks, but were constantly offering their dirty paws with as much hauteur and nonchalance as if they were conferring a vast deal of honor." It was reported the blacks could speak English as well as Indian dialects, and that they felt satisfied with their situation. Actually only a few black Seminoles were bilingual, those that did speak two languages became influential in Seminole councils.

Within Seminole society blacks occupied every different status, some were "more equal than others." Some blacks were born free, some were the descendents of fugitive slaves, some were fugitives themselves, some were interpreters and advisers, some warriors and hunters, and others field hands. Regardless of what their status in Seminole society, blacks felt they were much better off than in plantation bondage

Whites living near the Seminoles became acquainted with the Indians and their black interpreters and advisors through trade. Seminoles would come to trading posts and plantations. Many white-owned slaves had spouses or relatives living in Seminole territory. Whites would enter black Seminole villages looking for runaway slaves, which was a violation of the Moultrie Creek Treaty.

In 1826 Florida Territorial Governor DuVal told the Seminoles to return any runaway slaves, or the army will take them by force, "and in the confusion, many of you may lose your own slaves." The principal spokesman for the Seminoles Tuckose (TOK ko chi) Emathla (e MA he) (John Hicks) did not like the talk of the Indians hiding runaway slaves, he said this was not true, and he also complained that the white people had some of their blacks, and he expected them to be returned.

The legal mechanisms for settling these disputes over slaves between Seminoles and the whites were obviously not working. Governor DuVal suggested the government buy the slaves from the Seminoles, since individuals were prohibited from slave trading with the Indians. Governor DuVal felt by distancing blacks from the Seminoles this would help with the "Indian situation," since, he felt, the black Seminoles were a "bad" influence on their masters. The superintendent of Indian Affairs told DuVal this would not work, since agents should not be involved in the slave trade with their charges.

Florida agents were instructed to use due process if a white individual took a slave from the Seminoles. If the Indians held slaves claimed to be runaways, the burden of proof was on the white slave owner. After the Moultrie Creek treaty the Seminoles did return some runaway slaves, but for the most part the Seminoles refused to surrender the slaves in question before a trial was held. The Seminoles did not want to surrender slaves as a precondition for resolving disputes since they knew they had no rights in court. In John T. Sprague's, *History of the Second Seminole War,* he states, "The Indian, conscious of his rights, and knowing that he paid the money, though incapable of showing the papers executed under forms of law, as he had received none, and relying upon the honesty of the white man, protested most earnestly against these demands, and resolutely expressed a determination to resist all attempts thus to wrest from him his rightfully acquired property." There were so many claims being made on the Seminoles for returning blacks to whites, that the Seminoles began to believe the whites wanted all of their blacks.

Whites of course saw it differently. Plantation slave owners complained the Indians had too much due process and the slave owners had no way of redressing their grievances. White slave owners also objected to the fact they could not go into Indian Territory and claim blacks that were not claimed or possessed by the Seminoles. Another point of contention was some of the blacks the whites purchased from the Seminoles would escape and slip back into Indian Territory.

Governor DuVal suggested that the Moultrie Creek Treaty annuities be withheld until the Seminoles returned the runaway slaves. In 1828 the Indian Office put this into affect, but later reversed its policy and forbade such actions in the future. Local slave owners sought an adequate military force to recover their property from the Seminoles.

Slave disputes between Seminoles and whites were further complicated by the fact the interpreters in these slave negotiations were many times former slaves themselves. The blacks were hostile towards whites, and were constantly counteracting advice to the Indians. Sometimes Seminole chiefs would agree to a white demand in a council meeting, but later were talked out of this agreement by their black advisors. What was decided on how to solve the situation was to move the Seminoles out of Florida.

When Andrew Jackson was elected to the presidency, public opinion in the South demanded stricter control over the Indians. In Jackson's 1829 message to Congress he urged Indian removal legislation, he soothed the opposition by assuring them removal would be voluntary and peaceful. In May 1830, Congress appropriated $500,000 for negotiations on removal treaties. The "Oklahoma Territory" the area north of Texas and west of Arkansas was designated for resettlement. This area was considered the only place, at the time, where the Indians would not be in the way of the white man's expansion.

Floridians had been seeking removal for years. The reason for their concern was the absconding of slaves by the Seminoles, and the Indians' willingness to aid the blacks evade their masters. The Florida Territorial Government totally backed the white slave owners' interests. Acting Governor James Westcott asked the council to strengthen the militia because "we have amongst us two classes who may possibly at some future period, be incited to hostility, and…it behooves us always to be prepared."

Since being moved onto the less fertile Moultrie Creek reservation many times food had become scarce for the Seminoles. In 1831 a food crisis occurred and there were many starving bands of Indians preying on the whites' herds and provisions. The slave and the food situation lead Acting Governor Westcott to decide the only humane solution to these problems was to move the Indians away from the whites, leaving the blacks behind.

In 1832 the Florida Territorial Government prohibited black Seminoles from traveling outside Indian boundaries. That same year Secretary of War Lewis Cass instructed James Gadsden, a Jackson supporter, and the moving spirit in the Treaty of Moultrie Creek, to arrange a removal treaty with the Seminoles. Jackson acted on the removal of the Indians not because of the plight of the Seminoles, but because of pressure being put on the Government by white Floridians who felt the Indians were in their way. The Government though put lofty hyperbole on to the treaty negotiations saying they were doing this since the Indians were suffering in Florida. Gadsden was to persuade the Seminoles to move west. The startling aspect of this treaty was that the Seminoles were to become a constituent part of the Creek nation, sharing with the Creeks an allotment of land west of the Mississippi. This was clearly an affront to the Seminoles. The Seminoles had always had to fight the whites and now they would have to fight the Creeks as well.

Gadsden met with Seminole leaders at Payne's Landing on the Ocklawaha River. The first thing to be considered was the selection of interpreters. Gadsden brought Stephen Richards, the Seminoles chose Abraham, a "servant of Chief Micanopy (me KA no pee,)" and interpreter Cudjo (ku JOE.) Cudjo and Abraham were perhaps the most influential blacks in Florida at this time.

Abraham was much more than an interpreter for Micanopy, he was a trusted advisor. His English and mannerisms were those of an Englishman's house servant. Thin and over six feet tall with a broad, square face and a thin moustache Abraham had a countenance of great cunning and penetration. He always smiled, and his words flowed like oil.

Cudjo was a regular Seminole interpreter. His jargon was that of a black plantation slave, his demeanor was of meek attention. Physically Cudjo had a slight paralysis. It is said this made him feel more vulnerable. Cudjo was the first black to side with the government. By the time of Payne's Landing Cudjo was drawing a salary and rations from the Indian agency at Fort King (near Ocala) and perhaps living there as well.

Gadsden had two main obstacles to the success of this treaty. His first obstacle was in regard to slave claims. The second obstacle was convincing the Seminoles they should combine with their old enemies the Creeks. Gadsden said that even though emigration sounded bad, it would be better than staying under local jurisdiction and starving. Gadsden said the Government could not continue to feed the Seminoles year after year. He offered $7,000 to settle all claims with the Seminoles; many of these claims were for blacks. The Seminoles said that much of the property in dispute had been taken as reprisal for property that had been taken from them previously.

Gadsden, meeting with Abraham and Cudjo, decided to add $400 to the payment. This payment specifically to go to the two black men, a bribe. It is said Gadsden could not have gotten the treaty through without this offer.

The Seminoles thought all they had agreed to in this treaty was to send a delegation to the Indian Territory to examine the proposed new land. This group, on their return, to report back to the Seminoles on their findings then a final decision would be made. The preamble to the treaty read as follows, "…seven of the Seminole 'confidential chiefs' were to travel west to inspect the Creek lands, and 'should they be satisfied with the character of that country, and of the favorable disposition of the Creeks to reunite with the Seminoles as one people,' then the articles of the treaty would be binding." The question is who is "they" in the phrase "they be satisfied?" Did this "they" refer to the seven chiefs or to the entire Seminole nation? That was to be the point of contention on both sides.

Seven Seminoles, Abraham, and Indian agent John Phagan headed out to Indian Territory in the winter of 1832-33 to look at the land. The Seminole chiefs found the land to be barren and hostile in the winter, definitely unlike Florida. While at Fort Gibson, on the Arkansas River, Phagan and three other federal agents prepared a document for the Seminoles' signatures. The document stated the group was satisfied with the area, and that they would live within the Creek nation but have a separate designated area. The Seminole chiefs had no authority to sign such a paper. They had to report back to the Seminole councils. Phagan would not take a no for an answer and threatened to refuse to guide them home until they signed.

The group returned and reported to the council what they had seen. Chief Micanopy informed new Indian agent Wiley Thompson the Seminoles decided to decline the offer. Thompson informed them that the group had signed away Florida. He told Micanopy to prepare his people for emigration. Abraham brought this news to Micanopy, and returned with Micanopy's reply "The old man says today the same he said yesterday, 'the nation decided in council to decline the offer.'"

Indian Agent Thompson had served with Andrew Jackson during the Creek Civil War. He was a tall, powerful man usually called General Thompson, a title he received serving in the Georgia Militia from 1817-1824. He had also served for twelve years as a representative from Georgia in the House of Representatives. He gratefully accepted his commission as Indian agent in 1833. If he had known the difficulties and perils that lay ahead of him perhaps he would not have been lured to Florida.

The Seminoles that had signed the paper at Fort Gibson were ridiculed by all classes, male and female, for being swindled by the whites. Resistance sentiment was so strong the signatories feared for their lives. The Seminoles opposed vehemently living with the Creeks; they gradually began to separate themselves further from the Creek Confederacy. Though this separation process was almost completed with the Red Stick War, the Creeks were still including the Seminoles in some of their treaties even though the Seminoles were not signatories. The Seminoles had objected to the Creeks doing this since these treaties usually were about indemnifying American citizens for slaves taken by Indians as part of the Creek annuity. What this meant was the Creeks were claiming black Seminoles as their own. This further complicated Seminole removal.

It was clear the Creeks wanted to bring the Seminoles into their nation to dispossess the Seminoles of their large black population. The Seminoles feared this since the Creeks greatly outnumbered them. The Seminoles also feared that if they moved West there would be no justice for them if there were no separate Indian agent addressing Seminole issues. Washington continued to plan for combining the Creeks and the Seminoles on the same land and under one agency. The Seminoles said the slave claims of the Creeks had been addressed in the Payne's Landing Treaty, where the US agreed to pay for such claims.

Black Seminoles realized that the Creeks had a dubious claim on them. The blacks feared if the Creeks were to get hold of them the Creeks might sell them into real servitude or even sell them to the whites. So if the Seminoles ever did agree to emigrate to the West unscrupulous slavers with or without title could demand the return of the blacks. Or the blacks could be merely kidnapped. Black Seminoles were determined not to meet this fate.

A further complication came when President Jackson agreed with his Florida supporters that a good idea would be for the government to allow the selling of black Seminoles to whites. Governor Richard Call initiated the plan to sell the black Seminoles. He explained to Jackson if the Indians are allowed to convert the blacks to cash, it would be easier to remove the Seminoles to the West. Carey Harris, head of the office of Indian Affairs explained to the new Indian agent Wiley Thompson that this would not be an inhumane act since the condition of the black Seminoles, if sold, would not be any worse then their kind in the area.

Agent Thompson had his own concerns over the slave issue since he was fighting rumors spread by malcontent Seminoles that he had a stake in the sale of the black Seminoles. Agent Thompson feared that if a party of whites came with the permission from the War Department to buy the blacks, the blacks would immediately unite with the Seminoles. To overcome these obstacles Thompson proposed the government persuade the blacks to exert their influence on the Seminoles to relocate, assuring the blacks their continued existing relationship with the Indians. In the end Thompson was allowed to deny any slave trader entry into Seminole country by refusing them a license. Agent Thompson issued licenses at his own discretion.

Army officials agreed that black opposition to being sold to whites would give more strength to Seminole resistance to removal. Thompson asked chiefs leaning towards removal to do a survey as to the feelings of their people, including slaves. When the blacks heard of this compilation of their names and numbers they felt this was the first step in putting them under white control.

Most Seminole leaders opposed removal, regardless of whatever treaties were involved. Even chiefs that realized resistance to removal was futile would not voice this since many Seminoles were threatening the lives of any leader that complied with the removal plan. At this time Osceola emerged as a powerful resistance leader, and collected followers to his cause. In 1835 Osceola killed the leader Charley Emathla since Emathla was preparing his people for removal despite their opposition. Agent Thompson tried to reassure the Seminoles that the government would protect their property from the Creeks, if they moved west. He warned the Indians that their conditions would worsen in Florida without federal protection.

Micanopy was adamant about holding to the twenty-year plan of the Moultrie Creek Treaty; this treaty would not expire for another nine years. Other Indian leaders complained about the Payne's Landing Treaty, they said that it had not been explained to them correctly, they had only agreed to look at the land out West, not move on to it.

Abraham who had originally interpreted the removal treaties now counseled resistance to removal. Thompson felt this resistance talk was the result of John Phagan's actions (Thompson's predecessor.) Abraham claimed he had never been paid the $250 for his interpretation services. Thompson felt if Abraham had been paid this money, as agreed he would be more indifferent to the issue of removal. Thompson suggested Abraham only be paid if he shows more indifference to removal. Secretary of War Cass ignoring this opportunity to manipulate Abraham declined Thompson's suggestion, and said if Abraham was given the proper receipt for his services he should be paid.

Most blacks sided with removal resistance, and the killing of Charley Emathla by Osceola frightened the Seminole leaders leaning toward removal. Seminole communities all of a sudden were being abandoned in preparation for conflict. The Indians bought more lead and powder. It was clear trouble was imminent.

The eruption of violence in the last weeks of 1835 owed much to the black and Seminole alliance. The blacks were resistant to return to plantation slavery, and the Seminoles staunchly opposed removal to an unknown and desolate land in the West. This then began the Second Seminole War, the longest and most costly war in the US until Vietnam. It was further evident that the only way of assuring removal of the Seminoles was if they were allowed to take their slaves with them.

****

Anecdotes

Just prior to the Second Seminole War and during its first two years certain leaders were prominent. Micanopy was acknowledged as head chief, still his position was more nominal than actual. More able men surrounded him-Osceola, Abiaka, Coacoochee, and Alligator.

Abiaka (ah BEE ah ka) (Sam Jones)

Though his exploits were not as well publicized as Osceola's, Seminole medicine man Abiaka was important in Seminole history. Abiaka was a powerful spiritual leader who used his "medicine" to stir Seminole warriors into frenzy. His genius directed Seminole gains in several battles, including the 1837 ambush now known as the Battle of Okeechobee.

Abiaka nearly in his 70s was a well-proportioned small man with hair as white as snow. He was said to be as intrepid as a lion. Abiaka (Sam Jones) was a staunch resistor of removal. He kept the resistance fueled before and after Osceola's period of prominence and, when the fighting had concluded, was the only major Seminole leader to remain in Florida. Starved, surrounded, and with vengeance in his heart, Sam Jones would answer no flag of truce, no offer of compromise, or no demand of surrender. His final camp was in the Big Cypress Swamp, near the Seminole Tribe's Big Cypress community of today.

Alligator (Halpatter Tustenuggee) (hal PA ta tus tay NA gee)

Alligator was of the Alachua band. He was Micanopy's principal war leader, possibly his kinsman. Alligator was in his forties. He was well built, short, and a great warrior and talker. He was a shrewd and intelligent chief. He was fluent in English.

Coacoochee, (Wild Cat)

Coacoochee (co ah ko CHE) (Wild Cat)

During the first year of the Second Seminole War Wild Cat was not well known, but by the second year he became the most dangerous chieftain in the field. Born in 1810 he was slight, active, and well proportioned. He was attractive with eyes beaming of intelligence. His voice was clear and soft with ease of expression. After the death of Osceola in 1838, he became the principal leader of the Seminoles.

John Cavallo

Even before fighting began John knew most of the chiefs. During the conflict those relationships grew. Powerfully built and six feet tall, he was fond of silver armlets and elaborate plumed head shawls. John was an excellent marksman; he was courageous, and cunning. He was also known by the names John Horse, Gopher John, or Juan Caballo.

Osceola (Powell)

Probably the best known Seminole was Osceola, a head war chief during the Second Seminole War. He reportedly was a member of the Red Sticks. After the Creek Civil War of 1813-1814 many Red Sticks, including

Osceola and his mother moved from Georgia to Spanish-held Florida. The Red Sticks were absorbed into the Seminole tribe.

Six feet tall and leanly built, he was a spirited, strong willed, eloquent and courageous. Though he had no hereditary claim to leadership, his charm and charisma attracted the more hostile warriors to him.

The name Osceola appears an English mispronunciation of Asi-yohola, meaning Black Drink Crier. This name referring to the drawn out cry that accompanies the ceremonial drinking of the "black drink" (asi) used for purification.

Osceola had two wives and several children. One of his wives—Chechoter (meaning Morning Dew) was a descendent of a fugitive slave on her mother's side, the laws of slave holding traced children through their mothers. Thus she was considered a runaway slave, even though her father was Seminole. One day, while at a trading post with Osceola, she was captured by slave traders and taken to Georgia and sold. This was one of several incidents that made Osceola hate non-Seminoles and fire his resistance to removal.

CHAPTER EIGHT

The Second Seminole War

The Seminoles were determined to hold on to their beloved homeland. This determination would cost the Seminoles dearly in lives and homes lost, and it would bring upon them the wrath of the US Government. The Government, at the beginning of the Second Seminole War, looked forward to engaging the Indians. It wanted to flex its military muscle after the US military's near collapse in the war of 1812. After the war of 1812 the US Government was not sure it could repel a foreign invasion, and more and more states were seeking control of their own destinies apart from the Federal Government. By engaging in a war against the Seminoles the Government would unite the military and strengthen the concept of an all-powerful Federal Government. Between the issue of slavery, a government seeking power, and whites wanting to expand into Florida the Seminoles were caught in an ever tightening vice.

The US was determined to relocate the Seminoles to lands west of the Mississippi River. Osceola was vehemently opposed to removal, and advised the principal Seminole chief Micanopy to resist. Even though Osceola had no hereditary claim to leadership he was well respected by the Seminole leaders. Osceola sat close to Micanopy during councils, urging the chief to be firm against removal. Micanopy had much influence among the Seminoles. Micanopy, though, was a tractable chief and was easily convinced and influenced by others.

Indian Agent General Wiley Thompson was ordered to have the Seminole leaders agree to relocation and sign the Indian Relocation Treaty. Thompson declared "those leaders who did not sign the treaty would not be considered Seminole chiefs, and would not represent the tribe." Osceola did not like this at all. He defiantly strode to the table where the treaty lay and declared, "the only treaty I will sign is with this!" He plunged his knife through it. Osceola quickly gained recognition as a spirited, fearless leader and an eloquent speaker. Because of his refusal to sign the treaty of relocation, Agent Thompson had Osceola jailed in the spring of 1835. Osceola declared, "The sun is high, I will remember the hour. The agent has had his day, I will have mine."

This prophecy came true. After six days in prison, he was released when he appeared to give in to relocation. This was not what was going through Osceola's mind. Osceola sought revenge. The Seminoles were scheduled to move west beginning in January of 1836. In 1835 Osceola convinced the Seminoles to use force to resist removal and defend their homeland. On December 28, 1835, he and some 50 warriors ambushed Agent Thompson as he went out for an after dinner walk. Thompson was shot 15 times.

That same day, a group of warriors and blacks led by Chief Micanopy attacked troops led by Major Francis Dade. A group of 180 ambushed a detachment of 110 soldiers, led by Dade. The attackers hid in the grass and palmettos. They watched the trail where Dade and his troops were supposed to be traveling. The column of soldiers passed right by the attackers, oblivious to the fact they were there. The Seminoles and blacks attacked. Only three of Dade's soldiers survived, though they were badly wounded. Thus began the Second Seminole War.

The first year of the war was a complete failure for the US military. They had lost many men and had only killed 131 Seminoles (this including blacks) and captured 15 warriors. The new commander at Fort Brooke (Tampa), General Thomas Jesup retaliated by chasing the Seminoles for two years. General Jesup was a true Jacksonian with a long and distinguished military career. He had fought with credit in the war of 1812. He was a career military man serving his country for 52 years. His policies many times were not well received during his tenure in Florida or in the eyes of history, yet it is clear he was one of the most important white men involved in the Second Seminole War. His duty was to deal with the Seminoles.

In March 1837, Seminole negotiators seeking an end to the fighting endorsed an agreement entitled "Capitulation of the Seminole Nation of Indians and their Allies." This document stated that hostilities were to cease immediately and stipulated the entire Seminole nation and their "allies" would move west. It is speculated that "allies" referred to the black Seminoles. To ensure Seminole cooperation they were to hand over hostages to the US military to assure their compliance with the agreement. The Indians were to move south of the Hillsborough River and assemble near Tampa Bay no later than April 10. The government would pay the Seminoles for relocation; and they were to receive government rations before, during, and for one year after removal. Article 5 of the treaty stated, "Major General Jesup, in behalf of the United States, agreed that the Seminole and their allies, who come in and emigrate West, shall be secure in their lives and property; that their Negroes, their bona fide property, shall also accompany them West; and that the cattle and ponies shall be paid for by the United States at a fair valuation." The treaty appears to have addressed all classes of blacks among the Seminoles. "Allies" supposedly meant runaways, who had participated in the fighting, and free black Seminoles such as Abraham. Bona fide property meant those people categorized as Seminole slaves. Abraham's negotiating skill is clearly seen in this treaty. Abraham was hoping his family would live in freedom under this agreement. Micanopy signed this treaty on March 18.

By the 26th of March more and more Seminoles and blacks were coming to Tampa Bay. General Jesup realized the blacks arriving needed to feel secure in their position, namely that they would be allowed to emigrate with the Seminoles. But by the end of the month Jesup became overconfident stating he wanted the Indians and blacks to unite and bring in the blacks taken from citizens during the war. Obviously the runaways that had joined the Seminoles during the fighting were no longer considered "allies" of the Seminoles in Jesup's eyes and now faced return to plantation bondage. Jesup tried to have some of the more amenable chiefs agree to these terms.

Planters that had lost their slaves during skirmishes were pressuring Jesup to have their property returned. On April 8, Jesup made a secret agreement with some of the Seminole leaders, one was Coa Hadjo (KU ah HA joe.) The agreement was to bring in the runaway blacks. This was an unwise move on Jesup's part. Coa Hadjo instructed his associates to gather the escaped slaves. He ordered them to be held away from Tampa and the point of embarkation. Coa Hadjo felt this would make the blacks more comfortable and allow the runaway blacks to be seized without incident.

By now, there were troops going into Seminole country for the purpose of watching the Indians, seeing they stayed in the region assigned to them, guard against new hostilities, and hurry them on to Tampa. The troops were also to round up runaways. Many times the soldiers did not have to search for these blacks, since they would turn themselves in voluntarily. The blacks had suffered along with the Seminoles during the fighting, and many were not used to surviving in the wilderness.

More combative blacks refused to surrender. Militants such as Osceola supported their cause. When Coa Hadjo announced in council the runaways would be returned, Osceola angrily stood up and said as long as he was part of the Seminole nation that would not happen.

At General Jesup's relocation camp in Tampa things were not going well. Several Floridians arrived at the camp looking for their slaves. This began great consternation among the blacks. The blacks that were in the camp fled, and carried the panic with them. Jesup concerned with this tried to convince the rest of the Seminoles to come in, but to no avail. On June 2, a band of Seminoles, led by Osceola and Abiaka, forcibly abducted Micanopy, Jumper (Micanopy's advisor), and other Seminole leaders from the camp. Many warriors and their families left with them.

Jesup was dejected and he announced another plan. If the Indians would surrender the runaway slaves among them, the Seminoles could stay in a small area near the southern tip of Florida. Jesup's superiors refused to consider this proposal. Now the blacks and the tribesmen kept their distance from the army. General Jesup remained optimistic though and was certain he had captured all of the important black leaders while they were in Tampa. He was nearly correct.

By October 1837, the Seminoles wanted to talk. Jesup sent a large supply of white cloth to make truce flags. The meeting was held at a place south of Fort Peyton (south of St. Augustine.) Upon the arrival of the Americans, the Seminoles were flying a flag of truce. There were smiles all around by the Seminoles. They stated, they had done nothing wrong against the white man, and wished to make peace. Osceola was in attendance.

At first all was pleasant. Then the Seminoles were asked why they had not returned fugitive slaves to the United States. While the Seminoles were trying to answer, troops were signaled to come in. It is not the Seminole way to fight in such tight quarters, and against such great odds. They did not resist. The troops took Osceola, and 13 other chiefs prisoner, including Wild Cat (Coacoochee), Coa Hadjo, and John Cavallo. This deprived the Seminoles of Osceola, their major war spirit; Wild Cat, "the Napoleon of the Seminoles;" and John Cavallo, the only black Seminole leader not yet captured. Only Chief Micanopy and his followers were at large.

From a nearby Seminole camp, 71 warriors, six women, and four Indian Negroes were also taken prisoner. They were all marched to St. Augustine's Fort Marion. Osceola and the senior chiefs were given horses to ride, the rest walked. Osceola was not well, suffering from a severe throat infection, most probably strep (some say it was complications from malaria.) When word spread Osceola was captured under a flag of truce, sentiment turned in his favor, against his captors. Osceola aware he was not well spoke to Wild Cat on how to continue resistance to removal if something were to happen to him.

John Cavallo and Wild Cat were already planning an escape from the Fort Marion jail. The captives in John's cell had secured a file, probably from a sympathetic black on the outside, or perhaps purchased for a silver bracelet. In November of 1837, the captives were able to remove two of the bars on the windows and twenty people, including Wild Cat, his two brothers, and John Cavallo escaped. Meanwhile, the at large Micanopy, unaware of this escape, was easily found and escorted to General Jessup's headquarters. He came under a flag of truce. Jesup told Micanopy he was now a prisoner. Micanopy ordered his inner circle and their families to come in and surrender.

The remaining Fort Marion prisoners were shipped to Charleston, South Carolina. There, the Seminoles were treated like celebrities. Many citizens came to greet the prisoners cordially. Osceola was given the post surgeon to treat his severe throat infection, but he refused. He asked for his own medicine man. But, he did not survive the infection. Osceola was given a funeral conducted with all the honors and respect due to a distinguished warrior. He was given a headstone that read OSCEOLA, PATRIOT AND WARRIOR.

Colonel Zachary Taylor had now just arrived in Florida. Fifty-four when he reached Florida he had already earned the nickname "Old Rough and Ready," because of his dislike of pomp and circumstance and his willingness to fight. He was brusque and profane the kind of man enlisted men admire. Before Florida he had never organized operations except on a small scale. Though, he had put together plans of attack when he was out in the frontier that showed his ability to anticipate and think. Florida was Taylor's largest command. Taylor's plan was to push the Indians away from "every portion of Florida worth protecting."

In mid December 1837, Colonel Taylor and his troops were ordered to proceed southeast from Tampa Bay to search for "hostiles." He found both Seminoles and blacks that wanted to surrender in compliance with Micanopy's orders. Meanwhile, the escaped Wild Cat, John Cavallo and other warriors were heading toward Lake Okeechobee. Colonel Zachary Taylor left Fort Gardner, near the Kissimmee River with more than 1,000 men, heading toward the lake. The warriors avoided this large army by disappearing into the swamps. The warriors finally made it to the shore of the lake to fight Taylor's army. Swamps protected the Seminole flanks, and the lake protected their backs. Never had the Seminoles prepared their fighting grounds with more care. They situated themselves in a hammock with about a half a mile of swamp ahead of them. The swamp had five-foot high saw grass, the mud and water was three foot high. The Seminoles cut down a corridor in the saw grass for gunfire, and cut notches in the trees to steady their guns.

When Taylor's men arrived at the lake and began to fight, they began floundering in the mud, water, and razor-sharp saw grass. They had to travel through this to get to the warriors waiting for them. Every tree now concealed two warriors—one standing and one prone. Each was covering the other. Every rifle and musket had been carefully prepared for the first volley of shots. This was the most important volley.

Taylor's men finally got on to firmer ground and advanced more quickly. A volley of fire hit Taylor's front line at point blank range, the Seminoles always aiming toward the officers first. The first ranks of Taylor's soldiers, except for some officers, broke ranks and retreated. Another of Taylor's units arrived, exchanged fire, and attacked with bayonets. After 2 ½ hours of fighting Taylor's men found ten tribesmen and two blacks dead. Taylor's men had suffered heavy casualties. For every one Seminole killed, Taylor had lost 7 men. Taylor had not captured anyone. Yet Taylor declared a victory, and was promoted to General for his "victory" at Lake Okeechobee.

In early 1838 the whites were war weary. Now it was proposed the Natives of Florida could stay, as long as they stayed south of the Kissimmee River and Lake Okeechobee. Those Seminoles that had already been shipped to Charleston and New Orleans would not be returned to Florida but would continue their trip to Indian Territory. General Jesup wrote to the President "In regard to the Seminoles, we have committed the error of attempting to remove them when their lands were not required for agricultural purposes; when they were not in the way of the white inhabitants…My decided opinion is, that, unless immediate emigration be abandoned, the war will continue for years to come, and at constantly accumulating expense." General Jesup's plan was to split up the Seminoles and their black allies. With his proposal that the Seminoles could remain in their beloved homeland he hoped that would make them more agreeable in having their black companions sent west to Indian Territory.

General Jesup knew that the tribesmen would not capitulate until the black Seminoles did. In an effort to get "Black Seminoles" to emigrate West General Jesup issued an order saying, that all the Negroes who were the property of the Seminole Indians in Florida who separated themselves from the Indians and delivered themselves up to the Commanding officer of the Troops, should be free.

Jesup justified this offer of emancipation by explaining by taking the blacks from the Seminoles this would weaken them more than the loss of their own people. Also by not having the blacks in Florida this would discourage more slaves from running away from plantation bondage. Jesup said, "they should be sent to the West as a part of the Seminole nation, and be settled in a separate village, under the protection of the United States." Since the Second Seminole War had caused so much havoc among the Seminoles and the blacks Jesup's proposal and the security it provided by federal troops seemed attractive. Unfortunately the Secretary of War rejected Jesup's plan to keep the Seminoles in Florida without the blacks. Jesup was ordered to continue with Seminole removal despite the difficulties.

General Jesup now had a difficult situation, what to do with the hundreds of tribesmen assembled near Fort Jupiter who believed they would be permitted to stay in Florida forever? If Jesup told them the news they were to be removed to Indian Territory this could create new hostilities. He felt the best action would be to seize them.

On March 19, Jesup summoned the Seminoles to a council to be held the next day. The Seminoles did not appear and began to break camp. General Jesup ordered his troops to surround them. By March 23, 513 Indians including 150 warriors and 161 blacks were captured.

In a single stroke almost as many tribesmen and blacks were seized as had surrendered or been captured in the prior fifteen months. Though Sam Jones', Wild Cat's, and Alligator's bands were unaccounted for Jesup figured negotiations were the best step in encouraging these bands to surrender. Jesup sent Abraham and Seminole leader Holatoochee (ho la TU chee) to help Zachary Taylor negotiate with Alligator. Alligator and 88 of his people surrendered on the 4th of April. This surrender included John Cavallo and 27 blacks. Taylor reported to Jesup, "Alligator will send for Coacoochee" (Wild Cat.) Jesup was delighted.

By 1838 John Cavallo had achieved full status as a black Seminole leader. Like Abraham, he now realized that the war was impossible to win and cast his lot with the whites. During the rest of the Second Seminole War, blacks no longer played a significant part in the fighting. For the first two years of the war they had been prominent in major battles.

Now Alligator, John and their followers were marched to Tampa Bay to await relocation. Their trip to Fort Gibson (Oklahoma) via steamship was short and successful. There were 1,069 Seminoles including Micanopy and Coa Hadjo in that group. A large number of John's old associates had preceded him to Indian Territory.

When the Seminoles arrived at Fort Gibson they discovered the land promised to them was not available. The region between the Canadian River and its North Fork, extending west to the branches of the Little River was supposed to be their land. The Creeks had already occupied the area. The Seminoles decided to camp around Fort Gibson, drawing rations and waiting for new lands to be assigned to them. The Seminoles that arrived at Fort Gibson were tired and a dejected lot. They had been told in Florida to leave their possessions behind…that new ones would be given to them in Oklahoma. This did not happen. These new residents of Oklahoma realized they had been relocated into a strange place with no tools or land given to them to sustain them.

In May of 1838, General Zachary Taylor replaced General Jesup in the Florida command. Taylor encouraged some Seminole chiefs to return to

Florida to persuade the Seminoles remaining there to emigrate. John Cavallo wanted to return with them. When Taylor heard John wanted to go back with the chiefs he was furious, he felt John was a threat to the venture. These feelings probably stem from the fact John had been one of the leaders at Okeechobee.

John did make it back to Florida, and in fact was hired as a military interpreter. Meanwhile, General Alexander Macomb temporarily superceded General Taylor's command. Macomb had been authorized to begin the terms of Jesup's plan the year before…the Seminoles would be allowed to remain in Florida's southern extremity. In May 1839, Macomb announced the end of hostilities. Both sides hoped the hostilities were over. Medicine Man Abiaka (Sam Jones) and Otulke-Thlocco (o TAL ke THLOC ko) (The Prophet) counseled the Seminoles to retreat to the farthest reaches of the reservation set aside by the Moultrie Creek treaty. Chief Billy Bowlegs and other sub-chiefs followed Abiaka south, to Big Cypress Swamp.

In 1841 US Cavalry soldiers finally captured Wild Cat. Wild Cat at first refused to emigrate to the West, then he finally said he would. Not only was Wild Cat captured, but also his brother, an uncle, thirteen warriors and three blacks were brought in as well. All were immediately shipped to New Orleans.

Colonel William Worth succeeding Macomb as commander in Florida, had heard of Wild Cat being in route to New Orleans and ordered his return to Florida. Worth wanted Wild Cat to persuade his people to emigrate. When the ship holding the warriors returned to Florida, Colonel Worth boarded and told Wild Cat the fighting must end. He must send out men to encourage the rest of his people to emigrate. They would have fifty days to do this. If this were not done, he would hang Wild Cat and his warriors at sunset on the fiftieth day. Wild Cat said, "I feel the irons in my heart." Colonel Worth's plan for the Seminoles was to remove all the Indians in central and northern Florida and then remove those Seminoles that had moved south under Jesup's proposal. By the end of a month,

Wild Cat's entire band was camped, ready to emigrate. At that time, Wild Cat's shackles were removed, and he was allowed to dress in festive attire to greet his people.

Meanwhile, in the Big Cypress area, the Government sought to accommodate the Seminoles that had moved south and began building a trading post 15 miles up the Caloosahatchee River. While the post was under construction, Chief Bowlegs and two other chiefs led 160 warriors in a surprise attack on the soldiers at the post. These chiefs were afraid this Government post would intrude on their last refuge, and allow the military to impress more Seminoles into removal.

The Army spent another three years breaking up Seminole villages in an effort to subdue them. In 1842 the Seminoles denounced "the Prophet" as a coward. He had failed to prevent destruction of the Big Cypress villages. Bowlegs was now chosen head chief.

Colonel Worth in defeat finally felt it was not worth trying to round up the 300 Seminoles living in the swamps. He proposed to end the Second Seminole War by leaving the Seminoles south of the Peace River. This is what Bowlegs wanted. He came to Fort Brooke (Tampa) in August 1842, and signed a peace agreement ending the Second Seminole War. Bowlegs said, "I'm tired of wet feet—moving back to the hills."

Of all the conflicts with Native Americans, the Second Seminole War was the longest—seven years. It was also the most expensive. It cost some $20 million and the lives of 1,500 soldiers. Only Vietnam would be a longer war for the US. Ironically both the Second Seminole War and Vietnam did not result in a victory for the United States.

The Seminoles now agreed to a "temporary" reservation east and south of the Peace River. In an effort to avoid the smuggling of arms to the Seminoles by Cuban fisherman, the coastal islands and Charlotte Harbor were excluded from this new reservation.

Cattleman coveted this new reservation. They had taken up claims on the west side of the Peace River. Their claims came under the terms of the Armed Occupation Act. This Act, adopted by the Florida Legislature in

1842, granted 160 acres to homesteaders with a rifle. They had to locate two miles from a fort. Many families moved to the banks of the Peace River. Chief Bowlegs and his Seminole tribe were on the other side. More conflict was inevitable.

Billy Bowlegs

Billy Bowlegs was one of the most influential of chiefs in the period of the 1840s-1850s. He was a fine looking fellow with a demeanor of great earnestness. Though his name would imply he had a physical condition— bow legs, he did not. Actually the name Bowlegs is a mispronunciation of the name the French gave to him of Bowlek.

He and his Seminole brethren did not want to leave their beloved Florida. He sought in any way he could to make peace between Seminoles and whites to avoid conflict and removal. Though he would not bow down to threats or insults made against him or other Seminoles.

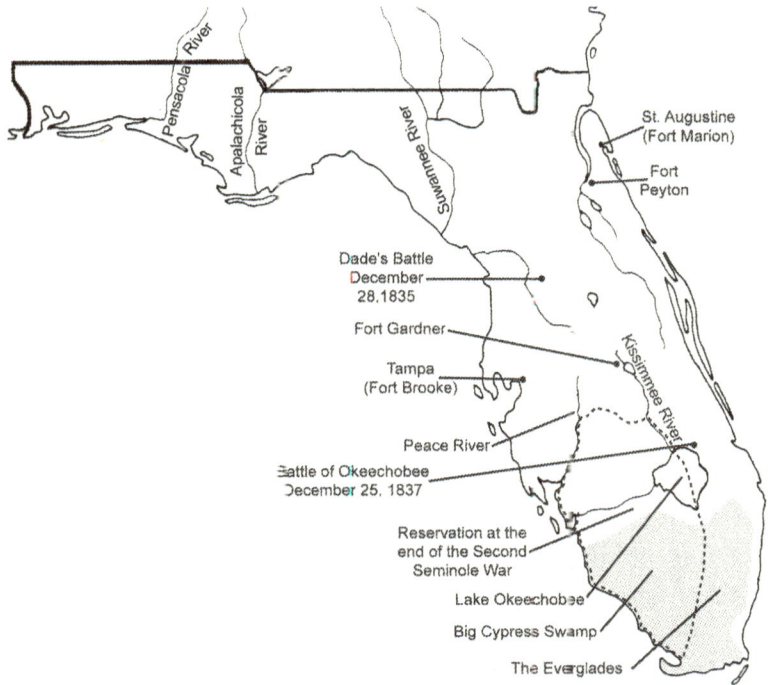

CHAPTER NINE
Indian Territory

The Seminoles dragged from their homes, and compelled to abandon their few possessions were faced with removal to a new and inhospitable home—Indian Territory. Bad weather, disease, and hunger many times marked their trips to this new land. Sometimes, if the weather was good and water levels were high the Seminoles could make it all the way to Fort Gibson, in Indian Territory, by steamship, more often than not they had to trek overland by wagon under horrible conditions.

When they arrived in Oklahoma they were destitute, cold, and hungry and were totally dependent on food given to them by the US Government. The change in climate, soil, and living conditions between their homeland and Indian Territory was so great and forbidding these bewildered and bro-ken-spirited people camped around Fort Gibson and received rations rather than venture out into the hazards of this new land. On top of all this hardship, when the Seminoles arrived in Oklahoma, they found the best part of their assigned land had already been occupied by their enemies the Creeks.

On July 14, 1842, John Cavallo's party left Tampa Bay, again, headed for Indian Territory. This journey was marked by hardship; they had prob-lems obtaining wagons, it rained constantly, and many fell ill. On his arrival in Oklahoma John found Wild Cat's and Alligator's people camped near Fort Gibson. They numbered nearly 1,100, and refused to settle among the Creeks. Instead they remained near the post on the land of friendly Cherokees. The Cherokees allowed the Seminoles to till the soil, but the Seminoles were discouraged from farming since they lacked tools and felt unsettled. An observer noted the Seminoles had some 1,000 blacks with them.

John sympathized with his friends Alligator and Wild Cat, who were living in miserable poverty. Micanopy, already in Indian Territory, was persuaded by John to visit Fort Gibson and meet with Wild Cat and Alligator. John interpreted at the council that took place. It was decided that the Seminoles should send a delegation to Washington to plead their case for a better life in Indian Territory. Alligator and Wild Cat would lead the group, Thomas Judge the Seminole subagent and John would accompany them. The Seminoles wanted land away from the Creeks, and protection for their slaves. In a month they arrived in Washington. On May 16, 1844, they applied for land apart from the Creeks. General Jesup, now living in Washington, welcomed the group at his home. He strongly supported their cause. Jesup wrote to the Secretary of War saying the black Seminoles had to be protected from kidnappers.

In January 1845, a treaty was produced between the Creeks, the Seminoles, and the US government. This treaty allocated land in the Little River area and granted the Seminoles local autonomy. The Seminoles were placed under the general control of the Creeks. A small sum was paid to the Seminoles for loss of their Florida holdings.

The treaty stated, "all contested cases between the two tribes, concerning the right of property, growing out of sale or transactions…previous to the ratification of this treaty, shall be subject to the decision of the President of the United States." The Seminoles took the word property to mean their slaves claimed by the Creeks. Naively confident the government would protect them they accepted the agreement. Federal law now bound Creeks and Seminoles, the Creeks being in control.

The Seminoles began to move from Fort Gibson to Little River. For sixty days John Cavallo used his wagon to transport people and their luggage. Moving to Little River helped the Seminoles since it gave them land to cultivate, but it exposed the blacks to increased kidnapping danger. They were surrounded by Creeks and were a far distance from Fort

Gibson. The legal position of the blacks was very confusing. When General Jesup was in Florida he had assured the blacks "if they surrendered and agreed to emigrate they would be settled in a separate village...under the protection of the United States, as a part of the Seminole Nation, and were never to be separated or sold." On the other hand General Zachary Taylor had told the Seminoles "those who surrendered and agreed to emigrate would be secure in their property, including their slaves." The Seminoles saw no difference between the two categories of free or enslaved blacks. Unfortunately other tribes and unscrupulous whites were always ready to intervene.

The Creeks claimed almost all the black Seminoles. They claimed that they or their ancestors belonged to the Creeks, and since the Seminoles were still considered part of the Creek Confederation, according to the Creeks, Seminole property was Creek property.

When General Jesup arrived at Fort Gibson in July of 1845, to plan for construction of new buildings, the black Seminoles reminded him of his promise of freedom. Jesup assured them his pledge was true. Several hundred blacks left their "owners" and sought sanctuary at Fort Gibson. Some of the blacks actually helped in building the new structures. Black relocation to the fort aggravated both Creek and Seminole alike. The Seminoles invoked the section of the 1845 treaty stating the President of the United States should decide such property questions. The matter was referred to the Attorney General, but the case dragged on for years.

As time passed, the black Seminole situation got worse. In June 1846, there was a slave raid at the Deep Fork of the Canadian River. Soon after this incident John Cavallo and two companions arrived at Fort Smith, Arkansas. They reported the Deep Fork raid to the Commander of Fort Smith. Because of this raid the trio requested land in Arkansas for the free black Seminoles. They felt that perhaps there would be more law and order in Arkansas. There was even talk by John and his colleagues of asking to be sent back to Africa so they could live in freedom. John a free black, according to a Seminole council decision in 1843, was in constant fear of being captured and sold into slavery. He wanted more than anything for the black Seminole situation to be resolved.

The blacks living at Fort Gibson were still being protected from kidnappers, but the fort could not hold everyone. In June 1848, a ruling by the Attorney General John Mason finally was rendered. The ruling stated that blacks should be restored to the condition they were prior to General Jesup's promises. President Polk agreed. Mason felt Jesup had exceeded his authority in granting the blacks freedom. Now the blacks that had considered themselves free for a decade were to be returned to their condition as Seminole slaves. The blacks would have accepted this, but conditions were impossible for this to happen. The Seminoles were surrounded by Creeks and could not protect their black comrades from kidnappings and fraudulent slave claims. The blacks faced their most feared fate, that is, becoming chattel slaves without rights.

Many blacks decided to leave Fort Gibson and settled near the present day Wewoka, Oklahoma, establishing a separate town. They knew they had to rely on themselves for protection and were ready to defend themselves. The Creeks complained these villages violated their laws. They ordered all free black Seminoles to leave the Creek Nation. The Creeks warned the Seminoles they would have to enforce these laws or the Creeks would have to intervene.

Wild Cat, who had never become a full Seminole chief, decided to broaden his constituency by taking command of the "black situation." He and John Cavallo became even closer because of this. Wild Cat and John now planned to leave Indian Territory. Wild Cat would unite disgruntled followers, including blacks, with other allies, such as tribesmen living in Texas, and then move everyone to Mexico where slavery no longer existed. John knew a land of liberty lay just across the Rio Grande and was glad to leave the Oklahoma morass.

In the summer and fall of 1849 the black Seminoles and Wild Cat prepared for the exodus. They needed arms, ammunition, and food. They purposely delayed the journey since a delegation was headed to Florida to try to convince Billy Bowlegs and Abiaka to relocate to Indian Territory. The delegates were scheduled to leave in the fall. Wild Cat and John Cavallo were asked to join the Florida party, both declined. They were headed to Mexico. When the Florida delegation finally left in October 1849, the emigrants hastened to leave, for their new land.

With a large number of blacks, 25 warriors and their families, some Creeks and Cherokees, Wild Cat and John led this group headed for Mexico and freedom. The group arrived on the Brazos River in the vicinity of the Kickapoo Indians. There they remained to make a crop. Wild Cat warned any whites or enemy Creeks who followed his band would be killed. Wild Cat wanted to entice as many as would follow him to Mexico. In Mexico Wild Cat would not have to contend with rival chiefs, and would finally be head of a tribe, thus fulfilling his ambitions.

Wild Cat returned to the Seminole Nation from Mexico in September 1850. He tried to convince the entire Seminole tribe to follow him to Texas. Wild Cat had a thousand Kickapoo under his command. He represented that the combination of the tribes could set up an Indian state in Mexico. Opposition from Seminole leaders stopped many from going. Wild Cat's return seriously agitated the Creeks. The Creeks fearing they would lose their slaves to Mexico. Some 600 Creeks set off to arrest Wild Cat, but turned around before getting to their destination.

Before the end of September Wild Cat left for the Rio Grande with a few Seminoles and about 100 blacks. Creeks pursued this group only to lose their blacks to capture by Comanche Indians. When the Creeks arrived and asked for their property back the Comanche's demanded ransom for the blacks. The Creeks paid and began to return with their blacks to Indian Territory. The blacks on the return made an abortive effort to escape. A bloody encounter ensued and many blacks were wounded. When the Creeks returned they had only sixty blacks in their possession.

Many other blacks tried to make it to Mexico and join Wild Cat, but their route was fraught with hazards. Comanches massacred many of them as they headed for the border and freedom. Wild Cat was now a force to be reckoned with and in March 1851, a Government commission was sent to talk to him. The Government was trying to figure out if Wild Cat was a threat to the US. Wild Cat very respectfully stated that he was only protecting his people from the harsh lands and hostile enemies that existed in Indian Territory. Wild Cat was happy, in Mexico he finally had the leadership and respect he had sought for many years.

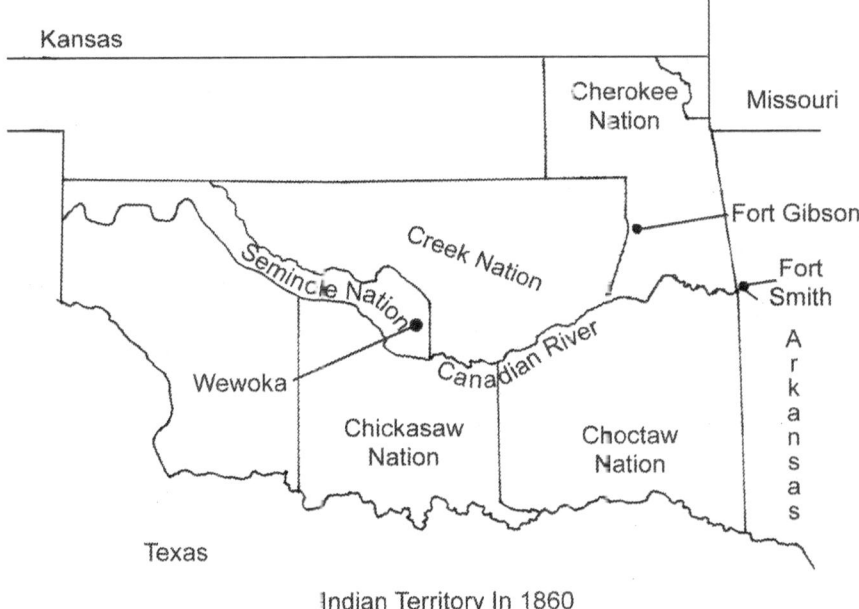

Indian Territory In 1860

CHAPTER TEN
Florida's Inland Conflicts

The years after the Second Seminole War were tense for the Government forces in Florida, the white settlers of Florida, and the Seminoles that remained. The Government knew it needed to somehow resolve the Indian situation. The white settlers were streaming into Florida under the Armed Occupation Act, and the Seminoles that had avoided removal were determined to stay in their homeland.

The Seminoles that remained would often travel from the interior of Florida, where they were living, to the Gulf coast to trade for goods. Many times this meant they had to pass white settlements—this was always a potential source of conflict. To deal with this situation the US Government decided to alleviate this problem by establishing a trading post so the Indians would not have to continue to pass their white neighbors. In 1849 the Government had its opportunity to establish such an interior trading post.

The Seminoles had been trading at a post located between the Peace River and Caloosahatchee River. In 1848 a mammoth hurricane hit this area and raised the water level by 15 feet. This trading post owned by Indian agent Kennedy was badly damaged. In 1849 Indian agent Kennedy received permission from the Government to relocate his trading post to Paynes Creek, near the present town of Bowling Green and the Peace River. This location was at the northern boundary of the Indian reservation. Kennedy transferred salvaged stock from the prior store to the new interior location. Soon after this transfer of goods, the Seminoles burned the empty old trading post. (This then came to be known as Burnt Store.)

The Florida legislature banned the sale of whiskey to Indians, in 1849. The Seminoles did not like this. On 13 July of that year, renegade Seminoles attacked settlers near Fort Pierce, killing one and wounding another. On the 17th of July, five Seminoles came to the new Kennedy trading post, offering deer skins for whiskey. Of course, they were denied. The upset (possibly drunk) Seminoles attacked the store. They opened fire on three clerks: Captain George S. Payne, Dempsey Whiddon, and William McCullough. Whiddon and Payne were killed. Their gravesite is now marked with a stone monument near the location of the trading post. McCullough escaped with his wife and child, though he was wounded in the shoulder and leg. The Indians set the trading post ablaze.

The attack resulted from the action of rebel Seminoles, one of whom had been outlawed by the tribe. Chief Bowlegs wanted to keep the peace, and sent a message to Indian Agent Casey. The message was a peace token left on Casey Key at the "Pescadores rancho" (fishing camp) of Felipe Bermudez. The sign was a bundle of white feathers with tobacco and beads. Bermudez left a sign the token would be answered at the full moon. Casey arrived at the rancho at the full moon and found Bowlegs' messengers waiting. The Chief's message said "the Fort Pierce and Peace River raids had been conducted by five renegades, and that he wanted to keep peace." Bowlegs asked for a meeting on September 18th.

Casey was well respected by the Seminoles—he spoke their language, and was always fair. He had made many forays into Seminole territory to gain their confidence and induce them to immigrate to Oklahoma, in return for money and gifts. It was said his mistress was Bowlegs' sister.

September 18th there was a meeting at "Burnt Store" to discuss the murders at the Peace River trading post and at Fort Pierce. Casey and Major General David Twiggs arrived on the paddle wheel steamer *Colonel Clay*. Chief Bowlegs and 37 warriors were waiting. Bowlegs and five of his men went on board and promised to deliver the murderers for trial—in one month's time.

In one month Casey and Twiggs returned to Burnt Store. Bowlegs turned over three Seminoles, and said another had been killed trying to flee, and the fifth had escaped. Bowlegs presented a severed hand as proof of death of the one murderer. He presented a bloody rifle as evidence that the fifth had been wounded while escaping.

Bowlegs said, "I have brought here many young men and boys to see the terrible consequences of breaking our peace laws. I brought them here that they might see their comrades delivered up to be killed. I now pledge you my word that if you will cease this talk of leaving the country no other outrage shall ever be committed by my people. Or, if ever hereafter the worst among my people shall cross the boundary and do any mischief to your people, you need not look for runners or appoint councils to talk. I will make up my pack and shoulder it. My people will do the same. We will all walk down to the seashore, and we will ask but one question—Where is the boat to carry us to Arkansas?"

The prisoners, handed over by Chief Bowlegs, were held at Fort Brooke (Tampa), but trial was delayed while they sent messages to family and friends urging them to emigrate to reservations in the West. Seventy-one Seminoles responded, and the prisoners were allowed to go with them as "guides." The prisoners were indicted for the murders, but they had already departed to the West, a month earlier.

Communication at that time was not good and even though the prisoners had been turned over to the US Army by Chief Bowlegs the Government was sending federal troops to Florida for a campaign to remove the remaining Seminoles. The plan for removal called for the establishment of a chain of forts, 10 miles apart. The forts would be located from the Manatee River to the Indian River—the northern boundary of the Indian reservation. The government felt this would protect the settlers and establish bases from which the Seminoles could be pursued and harassed until they surrendered. Work on the first fort started on October 26, 1849. Because of the incident at the Kennedy trading post it was decided to locate the first fort on an elevated piece of land about one-half mile from the destroyed post. The fort was to be named "Chokonikla," (cho ko KNEE kla) meaning burned house.

No fighting ever occurred at Fort Chokonikla, though troops did die from disease. Sicknesses, especially malaria, were constant problems. Ultimately sickness caused the fort to be abandoned in July of 1850. As many as 223 men, including a regimental band, were garrisoned at the fort at one time. The old fort, the Kennedy trading post, and the spot where Whiddon and Payne are buried can be visited at Paynes Creek Historic Site located outside the town of Bowling Green.

The Government's plan of harassing the remaining Seminoles into submission with the establishment of these forts did not work. These inland events of 1849 and 1850 did not immediately lead to the Third Seminole War, but definitely lead to further tension between the Government and the Seminoles. The Third Seminole War would be postponed until 1855 when conflicts arouse again over a bunch of bananas.

CHAPTER ELEVEN

The Third Seminole War

To encourage Bowlegs to relocate, Chief Bowlegs and seven sub-chiefs were taken to Washington, D.C. There they met with President Millard Fillmore and received medals. Bowlegs signed a letter agreeing to emigrate, but decided to move his people further into the Everglades. Trouble just seemed to follow him.

The Third Seminole War was started over the trampling of Chief Bowlegs' garden. December 1855, a fifteen man Army squad was sent out east of Fort Myers, to survey the Everglades area, and harass the Seminoles. Their orders were to "Explore the area, but make sure the Indians know you have no hostile intentions...The Indians will not attack unless provoked." This band made camp at a hammock three miles from the town of Chief Billy Bowlegs.

The next day four of the squad went to the village, and found it empty. Some of the soldiers took several bunches of bananas, and destroyed Bowlegs' garden. Bowlegs complained about their actions, but was laughed at and pushed to the ground. Bowlegs was furious. The next night, a war party of 30 Seminoles, led by Bowlegs, attacked the squad.

Soon raids by settlers and Seminoles began. June 14, 1856, a dozen or so Seminoles attacked a family building a house outside of Fort Meade. The settlers fired their rifles from chinks in the house, and killed one Seminole. Frustrated the Seminoles killed 12 horses. Two boys alerted the fort of the attack, and seven men mounted their horses and rushed to the scene. They followed the Seminoles to a hammock and fought them in hand to hand combat. One of the Seminole's throats was cut. With this, the Seminoles fled, carrying their wounded with them. Two soldiers were killed and three were wounded.

News of the fight got to Fort Fraser and the militia was sent to chase the Seminoles. The Seminoles gathered reinforcements and took defensive positions in the swamps and along the Peace River The militia found the Seminoles on June 16. The enraged militiamen charged ahead, chasing the Seminoles across the Peace River. Many Seminoles died in the River, including Oscen Tustenuggee, the Seminole war captain. The Seminoles returned fire from across the river, killing two and wounding three. The militia withdrew, and they were joined by a larger detachment. They pursued the Seminoles, but could not overtake them. Some 20 Seminoles were killed in the engagement. With the death of Tustenuggee, the Seminoles lost their desire to fight. Minor skirmishes continued for another year, but Billy Bowlegs realized the end had come.

The Army sent search parties to capture Bowlegs, but they gave up after floundering for weeks in saw grass and muck. The US Army also had other potential conflicts on its mind… the winds of war between the North and the South were beginning to blow.

Finally, 1858 marked the end of the Third Seminole War. Contact was made with Bowlegs through his niece, Polly, and Chief Bowlegs agreed to immigrate to Indian Territory. Forty Seminoles and four Creeks, headed by Chief John Jumper, were brought from Arkansas to assure Bowlegs things were not that bad out West.

Indian commissioners offered $6,500 to Bowlegs, $1,000 to each of the sub-chiefs, $500 to each warrior and $100 for each woman and child who would emigrate. Bowlegs persuaded 125 of his people to join him in immigrating to Kansas. In December of that year, Bowlegs was given $200 to return to Florida and persuade another 75 Seminoles to join him in Indian Territory.

Army records show Bowlegs was a Seminole chief that supported and fought for the Union in the Civil War. Some Seminoles and other tribes joined Confederate forces. In 1861 three battles between the Union and

Confederate Indian forces resulted in heavy casualties on both sides. The Confederate Indian forces prevailed, but Federal Indian forces under the command of Captain Billy Bowlegs arrived to challenge the Confederate siding Indians in 30 actions in the next four years. Captain Bowlegs was "deserving of highest praise," according to Colonel Wattles of the First Indian Regiment. Before the war was over, it was estimated two-thirds of the Seminoles and all their Negroes were within Union lines.

1863 a smallpox and cholera epidemic broke out in the First Indian Regiment. Captain Bowlegs died in March 1864, from smallpox. Bowlegs principal chiefs wrote to President Lincoln to inform him of Captain Bowlegs' death. Said one chief; "Billy Bowlegs went into the Army to help his white Brothers and the government. He died in the service of his country. He left me here with our Agent to take care of the women and children." Captain Bowlegs is buried in the National Cemetery near Fort Gibson, Oklahoma.

Only some 200 Seminoles were left in Florida in the 1860's and they decided to retreat further into the Everglades. For two decades after the end of the Third Seminole War, the Seminoles disappeared. They came out to trade every so often at Fort Myers and other towns on the edge of the Everglades, and then would slip back into the swamps. The remaining Florida Seminoles never surrendered after the Third Seminole War, and to this day remain unconquered.

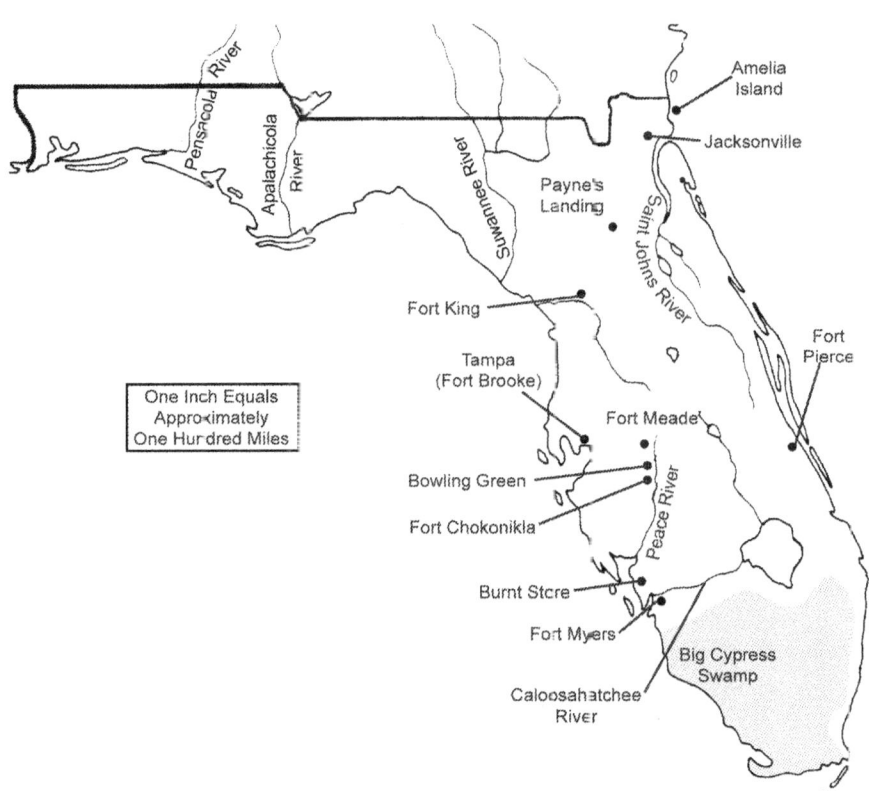

One Inch Equals
Approximately
One Hundred Miles

CHAPTER TWELVE

The Seminoles in the 20th Century

When the 1900s arrived, the remaining Florida Seminoles were living in small groups in the interior of the state. This area extending from about 60 miles north of Lake Okeechobee, to an area just south of the present Miami. The villages went from the present towns of Fort Myers/Naples on the west, to the present town of Davie on the east. The territory they occupied was almost the same territory inhabited by the earlier tribe of Calusa.

Now the Seminoles no longer had to face military action, or the threat of removal, but now the challenge was how to make a living, and how to maintain tribal unity among the scattered groups. This was complicated since there were two linguistic groups—Muskogee and Mikasuki.

The Seminoles were able to grow their own food on the highlands in the swamps—hammocks. They also hunted and fished. But, as the 20th century advanced, they wanted more manufactured goods, this meant they needed to figure out a way to make money. In the early 20th century, there was a great demand by designers and manufacturers of clothing, shoes and handbags for otter pelts, feathers, and alligator hides The Seminoles lived among these animals and were able to provide these goods. They realized the fashion industry would be the answer to their money needs.

But changes were occurring. In 1905 the Florida state legislature voted to drain the swampy Everglades, bringing this water to the coasts for drinking. A system of canals was created to accomplish this goal. This had an adverse affect on the environment of the Everglades, and its wildlife. Florida put in rail lines to improve access in southern Florida. This caused population growth on the coasts, and allowed ranchers and farmers to move to the interior. They began to clear and fence land for citrus groves and cattle. The Seminoles now faced being cut off from much of the land they had been occupying. In the 1920s a land boom in Florida brought with it new settlers, homeowners, and developers into the interior. The state also started an extensive highway building program that brought in more people.

In 1911 the Bureau of Indian Affairs (BIA) realized the plight of the Seminoles and set up two reservations—Big Cypress and Dania (Hollywood). On the reservations, the Seminoles would be protected from encroachment on their land. The Big Cypress reservation is located south of the town of Clewiston, near Lake Okeechobee. This reservation has some 43,000 acres. The Hollywood reservation has some 500 acres, and is situated west of the city of Hollywood. In 1926 the Hollywood reservation was deemed the site for the BIA's headquarters for the tribe. Some of the tribe felt comfortable moving to the reservation; many did not, remembering the attempts at removal in the 1800s. Many stayed away from the reservations, preferring to stay where they were.

By the 1930s Seminoles had more and more contact with the outside world. Some would work on the ranches of the area, some would do handicrafts, and some would be involved with beginning tourism—alligator wrestling. Yet the 1930s would be hard on the Seminoles. In the '30s restrictions were put on Seminole hunting rights. Also, as the economy of the US disintegrated, during the depression, so did the economy of the Seminoles. In the '30s the Seminoles gravitated towards Government lands seeking security and employment.

By the 1930s the Florida Seminoles had come to a crossroads—their continued existence as a tribal entity was in doubt. Cultural linkages that bound the Seminoles together were unraveling. Their economy was eroding along with the US economy. The fear was the Seminoles would merely join the amorphous mix of the rural poor.

In the '30s there were basically three socioeconomic groups among the Seminoles—1. The reservation families that had moved to the Dania reservation in the '20s, 2. The peripatetic agricultural and tourism related workers, and 3. The "traditional" families that remained in wilderness camps. The major obstacle to the Seminoles achieving economic and political parity was their lack of a tribal government. The problem, in the '30s, was only a fraction of the Seminoles lived on federal land and most had no interest in forming a tribal government, content instead to follow ceremonial "busk" (Green Corn Dance) social structures.

In the 1930s Christianity was rare among the Seminoles, instead there was still widespread participation in the Green Corn Dance. Thus medicine men and elders remained the primary political membership group for all but a few Florida Seminoles.

In 1934 the Indian Reorganization Act came into being and was enacted in 1935. What this act did was to provide for the ending of the sale of Indian lands, and allowed the organization of a tribal corporate structure to achieve economic independence and guaranteed tribal social and political self-determination through formation of reservation governments.

Also established in 1934 was the Everglades National Park. Congress specifically stated Everglades Park was not to conflict with the existing rights of the Seminoles. Though there would be limits on hunting, trapping, and other traditional Indian pursuits.

The Muskogee speaking Seminoles were most in favor of setting up government purchased reservations, the traditional Mikasukis did not. The Mikasukis preferring to live along the road that goes from Tampa to Miami—the Tamiami Trail. Some hard liner Mikasukis felt all the land south of the Peace River was theirs any ways. This idea stemming from the Second Seminole War. In 1935 the government began negotiating the purchase of land the Seminoles had requested. In 1935, the Government created a third reservation,…Brighton Reservation, on the northwestern shore of Lake Okeechobee. The state of Florida also designated 108,000 acres of land at the southeast corner of Big Cypress for hunting purposes.

By the 1950s the Seminoles had adjusted to their environment and were making a living in southern Florida. But something was missing—the sense of tribal unity. Mikasuki speakers lived at Big Cypress, Muskogee speakers lived at Brighton, and speakers of both languages lived at Dania. Further complicating the situation, many Seminoles were still living in isolated groups, the Seminoles were unorganized as a tribe. To gain economic and political parity with other residents of Florida they needed a central tribal organization.

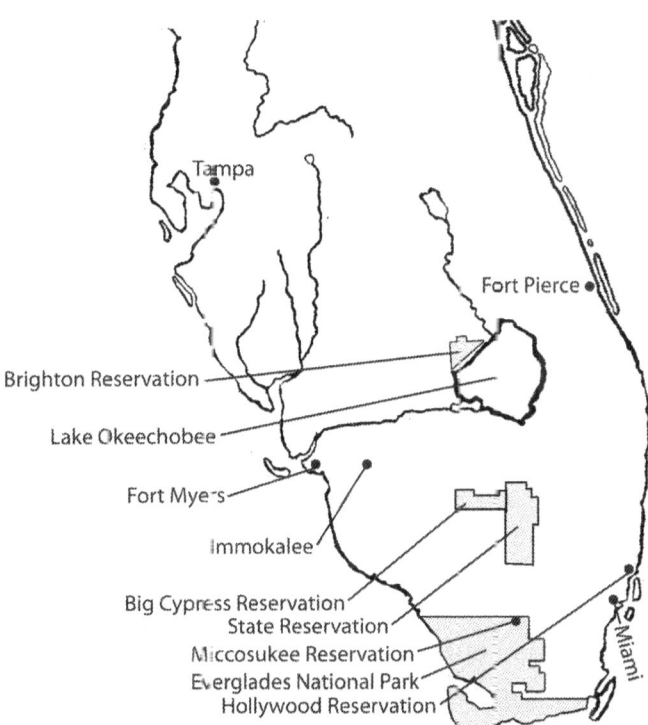

CHAPTER THIRTEEN
The Seminoles Create a Tribe

In the 1950s more and more Seminoles moved on to the reservations. By now Florida was having a tremendous land boom. In fact the 1950s saw Florida growing the fastest in the United States. Farms, orchards, and ranches were expanding, curtailing the movements of the Seminoles.

Yet, though more tribesmen were moving to the reservations, there was no tribal government to represent the Seminoles in their dealings with non-Seminoles. Billy Bowlegs, was the last person to be considered a chief to the Seminoles. Without leadership, the Seminoles had no say in local government, and no say about BIA appointments. The Seminoles used the Indian Reorganization Act (IRA), in 1957, to allow them to draw up a constitution of their own. They organized themselves as "The Seminole Tribe of Florida." This constitution governs the Seminoles to this day.

The constitution of the Seminole Tribe of Florida has two parts. One part provides for a council and the other for a board of directors. Adult members of the Tribe elect representatives for each of the federal reservations to the council and board. Each reservation has one council member and one board member. Only residents of each reservation are allowed to vote for that reservation's seats, but all members from all reservations can vote for the chairperson of the council and the president of the board.

Anyone over 21 can run for council or the board. They must be a member of the Tribe and have lived continuously for four years on one of the reservations. In 1967, the first woman—Betty Mae Jumper was elected as chairperson. Betty Mae Jumper was the first woman elected to chair any tribe in North America.

The Hollywood Reservation was designated as Tribal Headquarters. Both council and board meet there. The council is responsible for negotiating with local, state, and federal agencies. They also formulate and enforce laws. The board takes care of business matters for the Tribe, and is responsible for developing and managing tribal resources.

Though most Florida Seminoles have joined "The Seminole Tribe of Florida," there is a very conservative group of Seminoles that live along the road going across the southern part of Florida-The Tamiami Trail. They have named themselves "The Miccosukee Tribe." This smaller Tribe, some 500 people, has used the Indian Reorganization Act to set up their own political structure. Their headquarters is on trust land set aside by the Federal Government. This reservation is located about 40 miles west of Miami along the Tamiami Trial. Because the Miccosukee are of the same line as the other approximately 2500 Seminoles, they have the same rights to hunt and fish on the state reservation land that borders the Big Cypress Reservation.

The Seminoles that were removed to the West, in the 1800s, organized their own tribe known as 'The Seminole Nation of Oklahoma."

CHAPTER FOURTEEN
The Seminole Nation of Oklahoma

In 1856 the Seminoles of Oklahoma signed a treaty with the Muskogee Creek and the Federal Government. This treaty established the first Seminole Nation of Oklahoma. This nation was recognized as an independent nation within the US and under its protection. The land area encompassed the lands between the South Canadian River and North Canadian River; bounded on the east by a line where the present city of Tecumseh, Oklahoma stands, bounded on the west by the western boundary of the US in 1856...the 100th meridian. The Seminoles under the leadership of Chief John Jumper moved to their new land and established a community known as the Green Head Prairie. A council house was established.

When the War Between the States began, the Seminoles as well as other members of the Five Civilized Tribes (Cherokee, Choctaw, Chickasaw, Muskogee Creek and Seminoles,) took up arms and fought. The US government had agreed to protect the Seminoles from outside invasion, but did not. Before any battles were fought the Government withdrew all of its forces. This left the Indian Nation unprotected from invasion from the South.

Under the leadership of Big John Chupco (CHAP ko) one-third of the tribe sided with the North and moved to Kansas. The remainder of the tribe stayed with John Jumper and fought for the Confederacy. The Civil War devastated Indian Territory, and at its end the Five Civilized Tribes had to give up their claim to all their land in what is now western Oklahoma.

In 1866 the Oklahoma Seminoles were required to sign a new treaty. This treaty required the sale of the entire Seminole Nation land to the US. The rate of 15 cents per acre would be paid to the Seminoles. The Seminoles were required to free all their slaves and give them tribal rights. They were to give rights of way to the railroads; to make peace among themselves and with other tribes; and to help organize a state made up of the Indians in Oklahoma. The Seminoles were allowed to buy land sold by the Muskogee Creeks for a price of 50 cents per acre. This new land was the Second Seminole Nation in Oklahoma. This nation consisted of present day Seminole County and an additional 175,000 acres that the Seminoles bought from the Muskogee Creek.

When the Seminoles signed the treaty in 1866 the Government brought the Northern Seminoles (those that had moved to Kansas during the Civil War) back to their new nation and set up a new capital city. The site for the capital was Wewoka. 17 years earlier John Cavallo had established a town there. Wewoka means "barking water." The name comes from the noise made by a small falls near the settlement. That same year a trading post was built and in 1867 the first Post Office was commissioned.

There was a period of adjustment when both north and south factions of the tribe returned to the settlement. The Government recognized Big John Chupco as the Chief, though the majority of the Seminoles followed John Jumper. When an election was held John Jumper became undisputed chief.

Now the Oklahoma Seminole Nation has 14 bands (clans) each with two representatives on the General Council. Two of the bands are descendants of slaves who came with the tribe from Florida. Membership in a particular band is inherited through the line of one's mother. Each band meets once a month to discuss tribal matters of importance.

The Seminole Nation of Oklahoma has an elected Chief and Assistant Chief; they represent the Tribe as a whole. All final decisions regarding the Tribe are the responsibility of the General Council.

The religion of the Seminoles of Oklahoma is that of Christianity and Traditional Christianity. Traditional religion is also celebrated in the stomp dance. The stomp dance is derived from the Green Corn Dance. The Green Corn Dance was brought over by the Seminoles when they came from Florida. Seminole children are encouraged in school to study the culture, heritage, and language of the Tribe.

The Seminole Nation of Oklahoma currently has approximately 12,000 Tribal members. About 60% live within or near the Seminole Nation boundaries. Seven hundred live outside the state of Oklahoma the rest live within Oklahoma State lines.

CHAPTER FIFTEEN

The Florida Seminoles Today

The Florida Seminoles now occupy six reservations—located at Tampa, Immokalee, Hollywood, Fort Pierce, Big Cypress, and Brighton. The Seminole Tribe has more non-adjoining reservation than any other Native American tribe in North America. They have become excellent business people, and in the last 20 or so years have made great economic advances.

Today the Seminole Tribe employs over 2,000 non-Seminoles. They buy over $24 million in goods from over 850 Florida vendors per year, and the Tribe pays $3.5 million in federal payroll taxes per year.

On the Tampa reservation the Seminoles are involved in hotel and gaming businesses. They also have a Seminole museum and gift shop. On the Hollywood reservation, Tribal headquarters, they are involved in gaming, have a museum, a gift shop, and tourist attractions.

The Brighton reservation boasts aquaculture, arts and crafts industry, and gaming. They also own "Brighton Citrus." Originally a 40 acre grove, now it has expanded to 150 acres. The Tribe is looking to expand the acreage by another 85 acres—for a total of 235. In 1990 the Seminole Tribe purchased the leases on 1500 acres of lemon and grapefruit groves from Big Cypress Groves, Inc., and Garden Groves, Inc. On the Immokalee reservation, there are arts and crafts, gaming, and the Seminole Brand Rope factory.

At the Big Cypress Reservation, the visitor will find the Ah-Tah-Thi-Ki (ah-TAHTH-a-key) museum. This is a cultural and educational tool for Seminole and non-Seminole alike, well worth the trip. There are The Big

Cypress campgrounds, and Big Cypress Hunting Adventures. Available at Kissimmee Billie's Swamp Safari are airboat rides, swamp buggy rides, and the Swamp Water Cafe. Also located on Big Cypress are citrus groves and vegetable farms.

In 1995, 50 acres of St. Lucie County—Fort Pierce, was put in trust of the United States. This is now the sixth reservation of the Seminoles. Two dozen Seminole families will live on this reservation. They are descendents of Seminoles who lived in the area before there was a city or county.

Located in Fort Pierce, but off the reservation, is Micco Aircraft. The Micco Aircraft company produces high quality private aircraft.

The Tribe also provides many services to Seminole and non-Seminole alike. There is the Aviation Department. This is a Tribal owned airstrip located at Big Cypress. The Seminoles run WSBC Broadcasting from Hollywood. There are three sister stations at Big Cypress, Brighton, and Immokalee reservations. They have an Educational Division—education programs for Seminoles from 6 weeks of age to senior citizen. There is the Tribal Library System. These libraries are open to Tribe members as well as the public. The Seminole Tribe has a Water Resource Management Department. In 1987 the Tribal Council began the WRMD to protect and evaluate the land and water resources of the Tribe.

The Seminoles now move into the 21st century with their "Unconquerable" energy, sense of fairness, and finally a place and government they can call their own. As we enter the new millenium, the Seminoles will have a significant role in helping us understand the history of the past, and will be an integral part of shaping history in the future.

About the Author

The last three decades Dr. Sandi Towers has studied the indigenous peoples of the Americas, from the Alaskan Haida and Tlingit, to the Hopi and Navajo of Arizona, to the Quechua of Peru, to the natives of the Hawaiian Islands. A native of Florida, her late father, Robert, would always relate to her stories of the Seminoles of Florida—especially how they had never surrendered, and the fact they were unconquered.

Dr. Towers is an alumna of Pima College in Tucson, Arizona, Arizona State University in Tempe, Arizona, and Western State University in Fullerton, California. She received an Associate of Arts degree in 1972, a Bachelor of Science of Laws in 1976, and a Juris Doctor's degree in 1978. In 1982 Dr. Towers completed postdoctoral studies in international law.

Dr. Towers has traveled around the world to study and experience other cultures. She states, "the world would be such a boring place if we all were alike." Dr. Towers has lived in eleven states in the US, in England, Hong Kong, Mexico, and Colombia. She returned home to Florida, with her husband Dale in 1997, and now continues her research and writing from their home in Arcadia.

Dr. Towers loves lecturing and teaching others about the knowledge she has gained through her studies and experiences. "It is very important to me to inspire people to be the best that they can be." She now teaches sociology at Florida Southern College, and does lectures on the Seminoles of Florida for Edison Community College, the Charlotte County Historical Society, Warm Mineral Springs Historical Society, the Southwest Florida Historical Society, La Belle Historical Society, and local schools.

She states, "if I have learned anything through my travels and experiences, it is that we all hold to Universal spiritual truths and we are all basically the same no matter what corner of the globe we inhabit."

Appendix

HISTORICAL DOCUMENTS

I have added the Treaty of Moultrie Creek to let the reader see what the Seminoles actually signed. It is interesting how Article Four was repeatedly violated in the white man's search for "runaway" slaves. "ARTICLE 4. The United States promise to guaranty to the said tribes the peaceable possession of the district of country herein assigned them, reserving the right of opening through it such roads, as may, from time to time, be deemed necessary; and to restrain and prevent all white persons from hunting, settling, or otherwise intruding upon it." I have left the grammar and spelling as I found it in the original document.

TREATY OF MOULTRIE CREEK, FLORIDA
TERRITORY WITH THE FLORIDA TRIBES OF INDIANS
SEPTEMBER 18, 1823

7 Stat., 224.
Proclamation. Jan. 2, 1824.

ARTICLE 1. THE undersigned chiefs and warriors, for themselves and their tribes, have appealed to the humanity, and thrown themselves on, and have promised to continue under, the protection of the United States, and of no other nation, power, or sovereign; and, in consideration of the promises and stipulations hereinafter made, do cede and relinquish all claim or title which they may have to the whole territory of Florida, with the exception of such district of country as shall herein be allotted to them.

ARTICLE 2. The Florida tribes of Indians will hereafter be concentrated and confined to the following metes and boundaries: commencing five miles north of Okehumke, running in a direct line to a point five miles west of Setarky's settlement, on the waters of Amazura, (or Withlahuchie river) leaving said settlement two miles south of the line; from thence, in a direct line, to the south end of the Big Hammock, to include Chickuchate; continuing, in the same direction, for five miles beyond the said Hammock provided said point does not approach nearer than fifteen miles the sea coast of the Gulf of Mexico; if it does, the said line will terminate at that distance from the sea coast; thence, south, twelve miles.; thence in a south 30(c) east direction, until the same shall strike within five miles of the main branch of Charlotte river; thence, in a due east direction, to within twenty miles of the Atlantic coast; thence, north, fifteen west, for fifty miles and from this last, to the beginning point.

ARTICLE 3. The United States will take the Florida Indians under their care and patronage, and will afford them protection against all persons whatsoever; provided they conform to the laws of the United States, and refrain from making war, or giving any insult to any foreign nation, without having first obtained the permission and consent of the United States: And, in consideration of the appeal and cession made in the first article of this treaty, by the aforesaid chiefs and warriors, the United States promise to distribute among the tribes, as soon as concentrated, under the direction of their agent, implements of husbandry, and stock of cattle and hogs, to the amount of six thousand dollars, and an annual sum of five thousand dollars a year, for twenty successive years, to be distributed as the President of the United States shall direct, through the Secretary of War, or his Superintendents and Agent of Indian Affairs.

ARTICLE 4. The United States promise to guaranty to the said tribes the peaceable possession of the district of country herein assigned them, reserving the right of opening through it such roads, as may, from time to time, be deemed necessary; and to restrain and prevent all white persons from hunting, settling, or otherwise intruding upon it. But any citizen of the United States, being lawfully authorized for that purpose, shall be permitted to pass and repass through the said district, and to navigate the waters thereof, without any hindrance, toll, or exaction, from said tribes.

ARTICLE 5. For the purpose of facilitating the removal of the said tribes to the, district of country allotted them, and, as a compensation for the losses sustained, or the inconveniences to which they may be exposed by said removal, the United States will furnish them with rations of corn, meat, and salt, for twelve months, commencing on the first day of February next; and they further agree to compensate those individuals who have been compelled to abandon improvements on lands, not embraced within the limits allotted, to the amount of four thousand five hundred dollars, to be distributed among the sufferers, in a ratio to each, proportional to the value of the improvements abandoned. The United States further agree to furnish a sum, not exceeding two thousand dollars, to be expended by their agent, to facilitate the transportation of the different tribes to the point of concentration designated.

ARTICLE 6. An agent, sub-agent, and interpreter, shall be appointed, to reside within the Indian boundary aforesaid, to watch over the interests of said tribes; and the United States further stipulate, as an evidence of their humane policy towards said tribes, who have appealed to their liberality, to allow for the establishment of a school at the agency, one thousand dollars per year for twenty successive years; and one thousand dollars per year, for the same period, for the support of a gun and blacksmith, with the expenses incidental to his shop.

ARTICLE 7. The chiefs and warriors aforesaid, for themselves and tribes, stipulate to be active and vigilant in the preventing the retreating to, or passing through, of the district of country assigned them, of any absconding slaves, or fugitives from justice; and further agree, to use all necessary exertions to apprehend and deliver the same to the agent, who shall receive orders to compensate them agreeably to the trouble and expenses incurred.

ARTICLE 8. A commissioner, or commissioners, with a surveyor, shall be appointed, by the President of the United States, to run and mark, (blazing fore and aft the trees) the line as defined in the second article of this treaty, who shall be attended by a chief or warrior, to be designated by a council of their own tribes, and who shall receive, while so employed, a daily compensation of three dollars.

ARTICLE 9. The undersigned chiefs and warriors, for themselves and tribes, having objected to their concentration within the limits described in the second article of this treaty, under the impression that the said limits did not contain a sufficient quantity of good land to subsist them, and for no other reason: it is, therefore, expressly understood, between the United States and the aforesaid chiefs and warriors, that, should the country embraced in the said limits, upon examination by the Indian agent and the commissioner, or commissioners, to be appointed under the 8th article of this treaty, be by them considered insufficient for the support of the said Indian tribes; then the north line, as defined in the 2d article of this treaty, shall be removed so far north as to embrace a sufficient quantity of good tillable land.

ARTICLE 10. The undersigned chiefs and warriors, for themselves and tribes, have expressed to the commissioners their unlimited confidence in their agent, Col. Gad Humphreys, and their interpreter, Stephen Richards, and, as an evidence of their gratitude for their services and humane treatment, and brotherly attentions to their wants, request that one mile square, embracing the improvements of Enehe Mathla, at Tallahassee (said improvements to be considered as the centre) be conveyed, in fee simple, as a present to Col. Gad Humphreys. And they further request, that one mile square, at the Ochesee Bluffs, embracing Stephen Richard's field on said Bluffs, be conveyed in fee simple, as a present to said Stephen Richards. The commissioners accord in sentiment with the undersigned chiefs and warriors, and recommend a compliance with their wishes to the President and Senate of the United States; but the disapproval, on the part of the said authorities, of this article, shall, in no wise, affect the other articles and stipulations concluded on in this treaty.

In testimony whereof, the commissioners, William P. Duval, James Gadsden, and Bernard Segui, and the undersigned chiefs and warriors, have hereunto subscribed their names and affixed their seals.

Done at camp on Moultrie creek, in the territory of Florida, this eighteenth day of September, one thousand eight hundred and twenty-three, and of the independence of the United States the forty-eighth.

William P. Duval,
James Gadsden,
Bernard Segui,
Nea Mathla, his x mark,
Tokose Mathla, his x mark,
Ninnee Homata Tustenuky, his x mark,
Miconope, his x mark,
Nocosee Ahola, his x mark,
John Blunt, his x mark
Otlemata, his x mark,
Tuskeeneha, his x mark,
Tuski Hajo, his x mark,
Econchatimico, his x mark,
Emoteley, his x mark,
Mulatto King, his x mark,
Chocholohano, his x mark,
Ematlochee, his x mark,
Wokse Holata, his x mark,
Amathla Ho, his x mark,
Holatefiscico, his x mark,
Chefiscico Hajo, his x mark,
Lathloa Mathla, his x mark,

Senufky, his x mark,
Alak Hajo, his x mark,
Fahelustee Hajo, his x mark,
Octahamico, his x mark,
Tusteneck Hajo, his x mark,
Okoskee Amathla, his x mark,
Ocheeny Tustenuky, his x mark,
Phillip, his x mark,
Charley Amathla, his x mark,
John Hoponey, his x mark,
Rat Head, his x mark,
Holatta Amathla, his x mark,
Foshatchimico, his x mark,

Signed, sealed, and delivered, in the presence of

George Murray, secretary to the commission,
G. Humphreys, Indian agent,
Stephen Richards, interpreter,
Isaac N. Cox,
J. Erving, captain, Yourth Artillery,
Harvey Brown, lieutenant, Fourth Artillery,
C. D'Espinville, lieutenant, Fourth Artillery,
Jno. B. Scott, lieutenant, Fourth Artillery,
William Travers,
Horatio S. Dexter.

ADDITIONAL ARTICLE. Whereas Neo Matlila, John Blunt, Tuski Hajo, Mulatto King, Emath-lochee, and Econchatimico, six of the principal Chiefs of the Florida Indians, and parties to the treaty to which this article has been annexed, have warmly appealed to the Commissioners for permission to remain in the district of country now inhabited by them;

and, in consideration of their friendly disposition, and past services to the United States, it is, therefore, stipulated, between the United States and the aforesaid Chiefs, that the following reservations shall be surveyed, and marked by the Commissioner, or Commissioners, to be appointed under the 8th article of this Treaty:

For the use of Nea Mathla and his connections, two miles square, embracing the Tuphulga village, on the waters of Rocky Comfort Creek. For Blunt and Tuski Hajo, a reservation, commencing on the Apalachicola, one mile below Tuski Hajo's improvements, running up said river four miles; thence, west, two miles; thence, southerly, to a point two miles due west of the beginning; thence, east, to the beginning point.

For Mulatto King and Emathlochee, a reservation, commencing on the Apalachicola, at a point to include Yellow Hair's improvements; thence, up said river, for four miles; thence, west, one mile; thence, southerly, to a point one mile west of the beginning; and thence, east, to the beginning point.

For Econchatimico a reservation, commencing on the Chatahoochie, one mile below Econchatimico's house; thence, up said river, for four miles; thence, one mile, west; thence, southerly, to a point one mile west of the beginning; thence, east, to the beginning point.

The United States promise to guaranty the peaceable possession of the said reservations, as defined, to the aforesaid chiefs and their descendents only, so long as they shall continue to occupy, improve, or cultivate, the same; but in the event of the abandonment of all, or either of the reservations, by the chief or chiefs, to whom they have been allotted, the reservation, or reservations, so abandoned, shall revert to the United States, as included in the cession made in the first article of this treaty.

It is further understood, that the names of the individuals remaining on the reservations aforesaid, shall be furnished, by the chiefs in whose favor the reservations have been made, to the Superintendent or agent of Indian Affairs, in the territory of Florida; and that no other individuals shall be received or permitted to remain within said reservations, without the previous consent of the Superintendent or Agent aforesaid;

And, as the aforesaid Chiefs are authorized to select the individuals remaining with them, so they shall each be separately held responsible for the peaceable conduct of their towns, or the individuals residing on the reservations allotted them.

It is further understood, between the parties, that this agreement is not intended to prohibit the voluntary removal, at any future period, of all or either of the aforesaid Chiefs and their connections, to the district of country south, allotted to the Florida Indians, by the second article of this Treaty, whenever either, or all may think proper to make such an election; the United States reserving the right of ordering, for any outrage or misconduct, the aforesaid Chiefs, or either of them, with their connections, within the district of country south, aforesaid. It is further stipulated, by the United States that, of the six thousand dollars, appropriated for implements of husbandry, stock, &c. in the third article of this Treaty, eight hundred dollars shall be distributed, in the same manner, among the aforesaid chiefs and their towns; and it is understood, that, of the annual sum of five thousand dollars, to be distributed by the President of the United States, they will receive their proportion.

It is further stipulated, that, of the four thousand five hundred dollars, and two thousand dollars, provided for by the 5th article of this Treaty, for the payment for improvements and transportation, five hundred dollars shall be awarded to Neo Mathla, as a compensation for the improvements abandoned by him, as well as to meet the expenses he will unavoidably be exposed to, by his own removal, and that of his connections.

In testimony whereof, the commissioners, William P. Duval, James Gadsden, and Bernard Segui, and the undersigned chiefs and warriors, have hereunto subscribed their names and affixed their seals.

Done at camp, on Moultrie creek, in the territory of Florida, this eighteenth day of September, one thousand eight hundred and twenty-three, and of the independence of the United States the forty-eighth.

Wm. P. Duval, his x mark,
James Gadsden,
Bernard Segui,
Nea Mathla, his x mark,
John Blunt, his x mark,
Tuski Hajo, his x mark,
Mulatto King, his x mark,
Emathlochee, his x mark,
Econchatimico, his x mark,

Signed, sealed, delivered, in presence of

George Murray, secretary to the commission
Ja. W. Ripley,
G. Humphreys, Indian agent,
Stephen Richards, interpreter.

The following statement shows the number of men retained by the Chiefs, who have reservations made them, at their respective villages:

Number of Men.

Blount 43
Cochran 45
Mulatto King 30
Emathlochee 28
Econchatimico 38
Neo Mathia 30
Total 214

Source: Indian Affairs. Laws and Treaties. Vol. II. (Treaties.) Compiled and Edited by Charles J. Kappler, LL. M.,

Clerk to the Senate Committee on Indian Affairs. Washington: Government Printing Office. 1904.

****

Here in the Treaty of Payne's Landing we see the concern of the US Government as to the slave issue. In Article Six, we find an interesting choice of words, "The Seminoles being anxious to be relieved from repeated vexatious demands for slaves and other property, alleged to have been stolen and destroyed by them, so that they may remove unembarrassed to their new homes." I would say the US Government was vexed about the slave issue as much as the Seminoles. I have left the grammar and spelling as is found in the original document.

TREATY OF PAYNE'S LANDING ON THE OCKLEWAHA RIVER, FLORIDA TERRITORY WITH THE SEMINOLE

MAY 9, 1832

7 Stat., 368.
Proclamation, April 12, 1834.

The Seminole Indians, regarding with just respect, the solicitude manifested by the President of the United States for the improvement of their condition, by recommending a removal to a country more suitable to their habits and wants than the one they at present occupy in the Territory of Florida, are willing that their confidential chiefs, Jumper, Fuch-a-lus-ti-hadio, Charley Emartla, Coi-had-jo, Holati-Emartla, Ya-hadjo, Sam Jones, accompanied by their agent Major Phagan, and their faithful interpreter

Abraham, should be sent at the expense of the United States as early as convenient to examine the country assigned to the Creeks west of the Mississippi river, and should they be satisfied with the character of that country, and of the favorable disposition of the Creeks to reunite with the Seminoles as one people; the articles of the compact and agreement, herein stipulated at Payne's Landing on the Ocklewaha river, this ninth day of May, one thousand eight hundred and thirty-two, between James Gadsden, for and in behalf of the Government of the United States, and the undersigned chiefs and head-men for and in behalf of the Seminole Indians, shall be binding on the respective parties.

ARTICLE 1. The Seminole Indians relinquish to the United. States, all claim to the lands they at present occupy in the Territory of Florida, and agree to emigrate to the country assigned to the Creeks, west of the Mississippi river; it being understood that an additional extent of territory, proportioned to their numbers, will be added to the Creek country, and that the Seminoles will be received as a constituent part of the Creek nation, and be re-admitted to all the privileges as members of the same.

ARTICLE 2. For and in consideration of the relinquishment of claim in the first article of this agreement, and in full compensation for all the improvements, which may have been made on the lands thereby ceded; the United States stipulate to pay to the Seminole Indians, fifteen thousand, four hundred (15,400) dollars, to be divided among the chiefs and warriors of the several towns, in a ratio proportioned to their population, the respective proportions of each to be paid on their arrival in the country they consent to remove to; it being understood that their faithful interpreters Abraham and Cudjo shall receive two hundred dollars each of the above sum, in full remuneration for the improvements to be abandoned on the lands now cultivated by them.

ARTICLE 3. The United States agree to distribute as they arrive at their new homes in the Creek Territory, west of the Mississippi river, a blanket and a homespun frock, to each of the warriors, women and children of the Seminole tribe of Indians.

ARTICLE 4. The United States agree to extend the annuity for the support of a blacksmith, provided for in the sixth article of the treaty at Camp Moultrie for ten (10) years beyond the period therein stipulated, and in addition to the other annuities secured under that treaty; the United States agree to pay the sum of three thousand (3,000) dollars a year for fifteen (15) years, commencing after the removal of the whole tribe; these sums to be added to the Creek annuities and the whole amount to be so divided, that the chiefs and warriors of the Seminole Indians may receive their equitable proportion of the same as members of the Creek confederation

ARTICLE 5. The United States will take the cattle belonging to the Seminoles at the valuation of some discreet person to be appointed by the President, and the same shall be paid for in money to the respective owners, after their arrival at their new homes; or other cattle such as may be desired will be furnished them, notice being given through their agent of their wishes upon this subject, before their removal, that time may be afforded to supply the demand.

ARTICLE 6. The Seminoles being anxious to be relieved from repeated vexatious demands for slaves and other property, alleged to have been stolen and destroyed by them, so that they may remove unembarrassed to their new homes; the United States stipulate to have the same property investigated, and to liquidate such as may be satisfactorily established, provided the amount does not exceed seven thousand (7,000) dollars.

ARTICLE 7. The Seminole Indians will remove within three (3) years after the ratification of this agreement, and the expenses of their removal shall be defrayed by the United States, and such subsistence shall also be furnished them for a term not exceeding twelve (12) months, after their arrival at their new residence; as in the opinion of the President, their numbers and circumstances may require, the emigration to commence as early as practicable in the year eighteen hundred and thirty-three (1833), and with those Indians at present occupying the Big Swamp, and other parts of the country beyond the limits as defined in the second article of the treaty concluded at Camp Moultrie creek, so that the whole of that proportion of the Seminoles may be removed within the year aforesaid, and the remainder of the tribe, in about equal proportions, during the subsequent years of eighteen hundred and thirty-four and five, (1834 and 1835.) In testimony whereof, the commissioner, James Gadsden, and the undersigned chiefs and head men of the Seminole Indians, have hereunto subscribed their names and affixed their seals.

Done at camp at Payne's Landing, on the Ocklawaha river in the territory of Florida, on this ninth day of May, one thousand eight hundred and thirty-two, and of the independence of the United States of America the fifty-sixth.

James Gadsden,
Holati Emartla, his x mark,
Jumper, his x mark,
Fuch-ta-lus-ta-Hadjo, his x mark,
Charley Emartla, his x mark,
Coa Hadjo, his x mark,
Ar-pi-uck-i, or Sam Jones, his x mark,
Ya-ha Hadjo, his x mark,
Mico-Noha, his x mark,
Tokose-Emartla, or Jnc. Hicks, his x mark,
Cat-sha-Tusta-nuck-i, his x mark,
Hola-at-a-Mico, his x mark,
Hitch-it-i-Mico, his x mark,
E-ne-hah, his x mark,
Ya-ha-emartla Chup-kc, his x mark,
Moke-his-she-lar-ni, his x mark

Witnesses:

Douglas Vass, Secretary to Commissioner,
John Phagan, Agent,

Stephen Richards, Interpreter,
Abraham, Interpreter, his x mark,
Cudjo, Interpreter, his x mark,
Erastus Rogers,
B. Joscan.

Source: Indian Affairs. Laws and Treaties. Vol. II. (Treaties.) Compiled and Edited by Charles J. Kappler, LL. M.,

Clerk to the Senate Committee on Indian Affairs. Washington: Government Printing Office. 1904.

****

I have added the congressional address of Andrew Jackson in 1830; his address to Congress in 1835, as to the progress on the Indian Removal Act; and the text of the Act itself to highlight how solicitous the tone of the US Government was toward the Indians of the Southeast. The promises made by the US Government, if kept, would have lessened the hardships forced on the Indians upon relocation, but still would not have corrected the injustice of removal from their native lands. I have left the grammar and spelling as found in the original documents.

President Andrew Jackson's Case
for the Removal Act
First Annual Message to Congress, 8 December 1830

It gives me pleasure to announce to Congress that the benevolent policy of the Government, steadily pursued for nearly thirty years, in relation to the removal of the Indians beyond the white settlements is approaching to a happy consummation. Two important tribes have accepted the provision made for their removal at the last session of Congress, and it is believed that their example will induce the remaining tribes also to seek the same obvious advantages.

The consequences of a speedy removal will be important to the United States, to individual States, and to the Indians themselves. The pecuniary advantages, which it promises to the Government, are the least of its recommendations. It puts an end to all possible danger of collision between the authorities of the General and State Governments on account of the Indians. It will place a dense and civilized population in large tracts of country now occupied by a few savage hunters. By opening the whole territory between Tennessee on the north and Louisiana on the south to the settlement of the whites it will incalculably strengthen the southwestern frontier and render the adjacent States strong enough to repel future invasions without remote aid. It will relieve the whole State of Mississippi and the western part of Alabama of Indian occupancy, and enable those States to advance rapidly in population, wealth, and power. It will separate the Indians from immediate contact with settlements of whites; free them from the power of the States; enable them to pursue happiness in their own way and under their own rude institutions; will retard the progress of decay, which is lessening their numbers, and perhaps cause them gradually, under the protection of the Government and through the influence of good counsels, to cast off their savage habits and become an interesting, civilized, and Christian community. These consequences, some of them so certain and the rest so probable, make the complete execution of the plan sanctioned by Congress at their last session an object of much solicitude.

Toward the aborigines of the country no one can indulge a more friendly feeling than myself, or would go further in attempting to reclaim them from their wandering habits and make them a happy, prosperous people. I have endeavored to impress upon them my own solemn convictions of the duties and powers of the General Government in relation to the State authorities. For the justice of the laws passed by the States within the scope of their reserved powers they are not responsible to this Government. As individuals we may entertain and express our opinions of their acts, but as a Government we have as little right to control them as we have to prescribe laws for other nations.

With a full understanding of the subject, the Choctaw and the Chickasaw tribes have with great unanimity determined to avail themselves of the liberal offers presented by the act of Congress, and have agreed to remove beyond the Mississippi River.

Treaties have been made with them, which in due season will be submitted for consideration. In negotiating these treaties they were made to understand their true condition, and they have preferred maintaining their independence in the Western forests to submitting to the laws of the States in which they now reside. These treaties, being probably the last, which will ever be made with them, are characterized by great liberality on the part of the Government. They give the Indians a liberal sum in consideration of their removal, and comfortable subsistence on their arrival at their new homes. If it be their real interest to maintain a separate existence, they will there be at liberty to do so without the inconveniences and vexations to which they would unavoidably have been subject in Alabama and Mississippi.

Humanity has often wept over the fate of the aborigines of this country, and Philanthropy has been long busily employed in devising means to avert it, but its progress has never for a moment been arrested, and one by one have many powerful tribes disappeared from the earth. To follow to the tomb the last of his race and to tread on the graves of extinct nations excite melancholy reflections. But true philanthropy reconciles the mind to these vicissitudes as it does to the extinction of one generation to make room for another. In the monuments and fortresses of an unknown people, spread over the extensive regions of the West, we behold the memorials of a once powerful race, which was exterminated or has disappeared to make room for the existing savage tribes. Nor is there anything in this which, upon a comprehensive view of the general interests of the human race, is to be regretted. Philanthropy could not wish to see this continent restored to the conditions in which it was found by our forefathers. What good man would prefer a country covered with forests and ranged by a few thousand savages to our extensive Republic, studded with cities, towns, and prosperous farms, embellished with all the improvements which art can devise or industry execute, occupied by more than 12,000,000 happy people, and filled with all the blessings of liberty, civilization, and religion?

The present policy of the Government is but a continuation of the same progressive change by a milder process. The tribes which occupied the countries now constituting the Eastern States were annihilated or have melted away to make room for the whites. The waves of population and civilization are rolling to the westward, and we now propose to acquire the countries occupied by the red men of the South and West by a fair exchange, and, at the expense of the United States, to send them to a land where their existence may be prolonged and perhaps made perpetual. Doubtless it will be painful to leave the graves of their fathers; but what do they more than our ancestors did or than our children are now doing? To better their condition in an unknown land our forefathers left all that was dear in earthly objects. Our children by thousands yearly leave the land of their birth to seek new homes in distant regions. Does Humanity weep at these painful separations from everything, animate and inanimate, with which the young heart has become entwined? Far from it. It is rather a source of joy that our country affords scope where our young population may range unconstrained in body or in mind, developing the power and faculties of man in their highest perfection. These remove hundreds and almost thousands of miles at their own expense, purchase the lands they occupy, and support themselves at their new homes from the moment of their arrival. Can it be cruel in this Government when, by events which it can not control, the Indian is made discontented in his ancient home to purchase his lands, to give him a new and extensive territory, to pay the expense of his removal, and support him a year in his new abode? How many thousands of our own people would gladly embrace the opportunity of removing to the West on such conditions! If the offers made to the Indians were extended to them, they would be hailed with gratitude and joy.

And is it supposed that the wandering savage has a stronger attachment to his home than the settled, civilized Christian? Is it more afflicting to him to leave the graves of his fathers than it is to our brothers and children? Rightly considered, the policy of the General Government toward the red man is not only liberal, but generous. He is unwilling to submit to the laws of the States and mingle with their population. To save him from this alternative, or perhaps utter annihilation, the General Government kindly offers him a new home, and proposes to pay the whole expense of his removal and settlement...

May we not hope, therefore, that all good citizens, and none more zealously than those who think the Indians oppressed by subjection to the laws of the States, will unite in attempting to open the eyes of those children of the forest to their true condition, and by a speedy removal to relieve them from all the evils, real or imaginary, present or prospective, with which they may be supposed to be threatened.

Indian Removal
Extract from Andrew Jackson's Seventh Annual Message to Congress

December 7, 1835

The plan of removing the aboriginal people who yet remain within the settled portions of the United States to the country west of the Mississippi River approaches its consummation. It was adopted on the most mature consideration of the condition of this race, and ought to be persisted in till the object is accomplished, and prosecuted with as much vigor as a just regard to their circumstances will permit, and as fast as their consent can be obtained. All preceding experiments for the improvement of the Indians have failed. It seems now to be an established fact they can not live in contact with a civilized community and prosper. Ages of fruitless endeavors have at length brought us to a knowledge of this principle of intercommunication with them. The past we can not recall, but the future we can provide for. Independently of the treaty stipulations into which we have entered with the various tribes for the usufructuary *[?]* rights they have ceded to us, no one can doubt the moral duty of the Government of the United States to protect and if possible to preserve and perpetuate the scattered remnants of this race which are left within our borders. In the discharge of this duty an extensive region in the West has been assigned for their permanent residence. It has been divided into districts and allotted among them. Many have already removed and others are preparing to go, and with the exception of two small bands living in Ohio and Indiana, not exceeding 1,500 persons, and of the Cherokees, all the tribes on the east side of the Mississippi, and extending from Lake Michigan to Florida, have entered into engagements which will lead to their transplantation.

The plan for their removal and reestablishment is founded upon the knowledge we have gained of their character and habits, and has been dictated by a spirit of enlarged liberality. A territory exceeding in extent that relinquished has been granted to each tribe. Of its climate, fertility, and capacity to support an Indian population the representations are highly favorable. To these districts the Indians are removed at the expense of the United States, and with certain supplies of clothing, arms, ammunition, and other indispensable articles; they are also furnished gratuitously with provisions for the period of a year after their arrival at their new homes. In that time, from the nature of the country and of the products raised by them, they can subsist themselves by agricultural labor, if they choose to resort to that mode of life; if they do not they are upon the skirts of the great prairies, where countless herds of buffalo roam, and a short time suffices to adapt their own habits to the changes which a change of the animals destined for their food may require. Ample arrangements have also been made for the support of schools; in some instances council houses and churches are to be erected, dwellings constructed for the chiefs, and mills for common use. Funds have been set apart for the maintenance of the poor; the most necessary mechanical arts have been introduced, and blacksmiths, gunsmiths, wheelwrights, millwrights, etc., are supported among them. Steel and iron, and sometimes salt, are purchased for them, and plows and other farming utensils, domestic animals, looms, spinning wheels, cards, etc., are presented to them. And besides these beneficial arrangements, annuities are in all cases paid, amounting in some instances to more than $30 for each individual of the tribe, and in all cases sufficiently great, if justly divided and prudently expended, to enable them, in addition to their own exertions, to live comfortably. And as a stimulus for exertion, it is now provided by law that "in all cases of the appointment of interpreters or other persons employed for the benefit of the Indians a preference shall be given to persons of Indian descent, if such can be found who are properly qualified for the discharge of the duties."

Such are the arrangements for the physical comfort and for the moral improvement of the Indians. The necessary measures for their political advancement and for their separation from our citizens have not been neglected. The pledge of the United States has been given by Congress that the country destined for the residence of this people shall be forever "secured and guaranteed to them." A country west of Missouri and Arkansas has been assigned to them, into which the white settlements are not to be pushed. No political communities can be formed in that extensive region, except those which are established by the Indians themselves or by the Untied States for them and with their concurrence. A barrier has thus been raised for their protection against the encroachment of our citizens, and guarding the Indians as far as possible from those evils which have brought them to their present condition. Summary authority has been given by law to destroy all ardent spirits found in their country, without waiting the doubtful result and slow process of a legal seizure. I consider the absolute and unconditional interdiction of this article among these people as the first and great step in their melioration. Halfway measures will answer no purpose. These can not successfully contend against the cupidity of the seller and the overpowering appetite of the buyer. And the destructive effects of the traffic are marked in every page of the history of our Indian intercourse...

Indian Removal Act (1830)

May 28, 1830

Chapter CXLVIII

An Act to provide for an exchange of lands with the Indians residing in any of the states or territories, and for their removal west of the river Mississippi.

Be it enacted by the Senate and House of Representatives of the United States of America, in Congress assembled, That it shall and may be lawful for the President of the United States to cause so much of any territory belonging to the United States, west of the river Mississippi, not included in any state or organized territory, and to which the Indian title has been extinguished, as he may judge necessary, to be divided into a suitable number of districts, for the reception of such tribes or nations of Indians as may choose to exchange the lands where they now reside, and remove there; and to cause each of said districts to be so described by natural or artificial marks, as to be easily distinguished from every other.

Sec. 2 And be it further enacted, That it shall and may be lawful for the President to exchange any or all of such districts so to be laid off and described, with any tribe or nation of Indians now residing within the limits of any of the states or territories, and with which the United States have existing treaties, for the whole or any part or portion of the territory claimed and occupied by such tribe or nation, within the bounds of any one or more of the states or territories, where the land claimed and occupied by the Indians, is owned by the United States, or the United States are bound to the state within which it lies to extinguish the Indian claim thereto.

Sec. 3 And be it further enacted, That in the making of any such exchange or exchanges, it shall and may be lawful for the President solemnly to assure the tribe or nation with which the exchange is made, that the United States will forever secure and guarantee to them, and their heirs or successors, the country so exchanged with them; and if they prefer it, that the United States will cause a patent or grant to be made and executed to them for the same: Provided always, That such lands shall revert to the United States, if the Indians become extinct, or abandon the same.

Sec. 4 And be it further enacted, That if, upon any of the lands now occupied by the Indians, and to be exchanged for, there should be such improvements as add value to the land claimed by any individual or individuals of such tribes or nations, it shall and may be lawful for the President to cause such value to be ascertained by appraisement or otherwise, and to cause such ascertained value to be paid to the person or persons rightfully claiming such improvements. And upon the payment of such valuation, the improvements so valued and paid for, shall pass to the United States, and possession shall not afterwards be permitted to any of the same tribe.

Sec. 5 And be it further enacted, That upon the making of any such exchange as is contemplated by this act, it shall and may be lawful for the President to cause such aid and assistance to be furnished to the emigrants as may be necessary and proper to enable them to remove to, and settle in, the country for which they may have exchanged; and also, to give them such aid and assistance as may be necessary for their support and subsistence for the first year after their removal.

Sec. 6 And be it further enacted, That it shall and may be lawful for the President to cause such tribe or nation to be protected, at their new residence, against all interruption or disturbance from any other tribe or nation of Indians, or from any other person or persons whatever.

Sec. 7 And be it further enacted, That it shall and may be lawful for the President to have the same superintendence and care over any tribe or nation in the country to which they may remove as contemplated by this act, that he is now authorized to have over them at their present places of residence: Provided, That nothing in this act contained shall be construed as authorizing or directing the violation of any existing treaty between the United States and any of the Indian tribes.

Sec. 8 And be it further enacted, That for the purpose of giving effect to the provisions of this act, the sum of five hundred thousand dollars is hereby appropriated, to be paid out of any money in the treasury, not otherwise appropriated.

Taken from: The Cherokee Removal: A Brief History With Documents. Edited by Theda Perdue and Michael D. Green.
New York: St. Martin's Press, 1995: p.116-7.

****

This is the Treaty made between the US Government and the Seminoles of Oklahoma in 1866. Note the chastising language of the Government for some of the Seminoles siding with the Confederates. I have left the grammar and spelling as is found in the Treaty.

Seminole Treaty

(Articles Pertaining to the Freedom of Slaves and the Adoption of Freedmen as citizens)

Whereas existing, treaties between the United States and the Seminole Nation are insufficient to meet their mutual necessities; and

Whereas the Seminole Nation made a treaty with the so-called Confederate States, August 1st, 1861, whereby they threw off their allegiance to the United States, and unsettled their treaty relations with the United States, and thereby incurred the liability of forfeiture of all lands and other property held by grant or gift of the United States; and whereas a treaty of peace and amity was entered into between the United States and the Seminole and other tribes at Fort Smith, September 13 [10,] 1865,a whereby the Seminoles revoked, canceled. and repudiated the said treaty with the so-called Confederate States; and whereas the United States, through its commissioners, in said treaty of peace promised to enter into treaty with the Seminole Nation to arrange and settle all questions relating to and growing out of said treaty with the so-called Confederate States; and whereas the United States, in view of said treaty of the Seminole Nation with the enemies of the Government of the United States, and the consequent liabilities of said Seminole Nation, and in view of its urgent necessities for more lands in the Indian Territory, requires a cession by said Seminole Nation of part of its present reservation, and is willing to pay therefor a reasonable price, while at the same time providing new and adequate land for them:

Now, therefore, the United States, by its commissioners aforesaid, and the above-named delegates of the Seminole Nation, the day and year above written, mutually stipulate and agree, on behalf of the respective parties, as follows, to wit;

ARTICLE 1. There shall be perpetual peace between the United States and the Seminole Nation, and the Seminoles agree to be and remain firm allies of the United States, and always faithfully aid the Government thereof to suppress insurrection and put down its enemies. The Seminoles also agree to remain at peace with all other Indian tribes and with themselves. In return for these pledges of peace and friendship, the United States guarantee them quiet possession of their country, and protection against hostilities on the part of other tribes; and, in the event of such hostilities, that the tribe commencing and prosecuting the same shall make just reparation therefor. Therefore the Seminoles agree to a military occupation of their country at the option and expense of the United States. A general amnesty of all past offences against the laws of the United States, committed by any member of the Seminole Nation, is hereby declared; and the Seminoles, anxious for the restoration of kind and friendly feelings among themselves, do hereby declare an amnesty for all past offenses against their government, and no Indian or Indians shall be proscribed or any act of forfeiture or confiscation passed against those who have remained friendly to or taken up arms against the United States, but they shall enjoy equal privileges with other members of said tribe, and all laws heretofore passed inconsistent herewith are hereby declared inoperative.

ARTICLE 2. The Seminole Nation covenant that henceforth in said nation slavery shall not exist, nor involuntary servitude, except for and in punishment of crime, whereof the offending party shall first have been duly convicted in accordance with law, applicable to all the members of said nation. And inasmuch as there are among the Seminoles many persons of African descent and blood, who have no interest or property in the soil, and no recognized civil rights it is stipulated that hereafter these persons and their descendants, and such other of the same race as shall be permitted by said nation to settle there, shall have and enjoy all the rights of native citizens, and the laws of said nation shall be equally binding upon all persons of whatever race or color, who may be adopted as citizens or members of said tribe.

ARTICLE 3. In compliance with the desire of the United States to locate other Indians and freedmen thereon, the Seminoles cede and convey to the United States their entire domain, being the tract of land ceded to the Seminole Indians by the Creek Nation under the provisions of article first, (1st,) treaty of the United States with the Creeks and Seminoles, made and concluded at Washington, D. C., August 7, 1856. In consideration of said grant and cession of their lands, estimated at two million one hundred and sixty-nine thousand and eighty (2,169,080) acres, the United States agree to pay said Seminole Nation the sum of three hundred and twenty-five thousand three hundred and sixty-two ($325,362) dollars, said purchase being at the rate of fifteen cents per acre. The United States having obtained by grant of the Creek Nation the westerly half of their lands, hereby grant to the Seminole Nation the portion thereof hereafter described, which shall constitute the national domain of the Seminole Indians.

Said lands so granted by the United States to the Seminole Nation are bounded and described as follows, to wit:

Beginning on the Canadian River where the line dividing the Creek lands according to the terms of their sale to the United States by their treaty of February 6, 1866,a following said line due north to where said line crosses the north fork of the Canadian River; thence up said north fork of the Canadian River a distance sufficient to make two hundred thousand acres by running due south to the Canadian River; thence down said Canadian River to the place of beginning. In consideration of said cession of two hundred thousand acres of land described above, the Seminole Nation agrees to pay therefor the price of fifty cents per acre, amounting to the sum of one hundred thousand dollars, which amount shall be deducted from the sum paid by the United States for Seminole lands under the stipulations above written. The balance due the Seminole

Nation after making said deduction, amounting to one hundred thousand dollars, the United States agree to pay in the following manner, to wit: Thirty thousand dollars shall be paid to enable the Seminoles to occupy, restore, and improve their farms, and to make their nation independent and self-sustaining, and shall be distributed for that purpose under the direction of the Secretary of the Interior; twenty thousand dollars shall be paid in like manner for the purpose of purchasing agricultural implements, seeds, cows, and other stock; fifteen thousand dollars shall be paid for the erection of a mill suitable to accommodate said nation of Indians; seventy thousand dollars to remain in the United States Treasury, upon which the United States shall pay an annual interest of five per cent.; fifty thousand of said sum of seventy thousand dollars shall be a permanent school-fund, the interest of which shall be paid annually and appropriated to the support of schools; the remainder of the seventy thousand dollars, being twenty thousand dollars, shall remain a permanent fund, the interest of which shall be paid annually for the support of the Seminole government; forty thousand three hundred and sixty-two dollars shall be appropriated and expended for subsisting said Indians, discriminating in favor of the destitute; all of which amounts, excepting the seventy thousand dollars to remain in the Treasury as a permanent fund, shall be paid upon the ratification of said treaty, and disbursed in such manner as the Secretary of the Interior may direct. The balance, fifty thousand dollars, or so much thereof as may be necessary to pay the losses ascertained and awarded as hereinafter provided, shall be paid when said awards shall have been duly made and approved by the Secretary of the Interior. And in case said fifty thousand dollars shall be insufficient to pay all said awards, it shall be distributed pro rata to those whose claims are so allowed; and until said awards shall be thus paid, the United States agree to pay to said Indians, in such manner and for such purposes as the Secretary of the Interior may direct, interest at the rate of five per cent. per annum from the date of the ratification of this treaty.

ARTICLE 4. To reimburse such members of the Seminole Nation as shall be duly adjudged to have remained loyal and faithful to their treaty relations to the United States, during the recent rebellion of the so-called Confederate States for the losses actually sustained by them thereby, after the ratification of this treaty, or so soon thereafter as the Secretary of the Interior shall direct, he shall appoint a board of commissioners, not to exceed three in number, who shall proceed to the Seminole country and investigate and determine said losses. Previous to said investigation the agent of the Seminole Nation shall prepare a census or enumeration of said tribe, and make a roll of all Seminoles who did in no manner aid or abet the enemies of the Government, but remained loyal during said rebellion; and no award shall be made by said commissioners for such losses unless the name of the claimant appear on said roll, and no compensation shall be allowed any person for such losses whose name does not appear on said roll, unless said claimant, within six months from the date of the completion of said roll, furnishes proof satisfactory to said board, or to the Commissioner of Indian Affairs, that he has at all times remained loyal to the United States, according to his treaty obligations. All evidence touching said claims shall be taken by said commissioners, or any of them, under oath, and their awards made, together with the evidence, shall be transmitted to the Commissioner of Indian Affairs, for his approval, and that of the Secretary of the Interior. Said commissioners shall be paid by the United States such compensation as the Secretary of the Interior may direct. The provisions of this article shall extend to and embrace the claims for losses sustained by loyal members of said tribe, irrespective of race or color, whether at the time of said losses the claimants shall have been in servitude or not; provided said claimants are made members of said tribe by the stipulations of this treaty.

ARTICLE 5. The Seminole Nation hereby grant a right of way through their lands to any company which shall be duly authorized by Congress, and shall, with the express consent and approbation of the Secretary of the Interior, undertake to construct a railroad from any point on their eastern to their western or southern boundary; but said railroad company, together with all its agents and employees, shall be subject to the laws of the United States relating to the intercourse with Indian tribes, and also to such rules and regulations as may be prescribed by the Secretary of the Interior for that purpose. And the Seminoles agree to sell to the United States, or any company duly authorized as aforesaid, such lands, not legally owned or occupied by a member or members of the Seminole Nation lying along the line of said contemplated railroad, not exceeding on each side thereof a belt or strip of land three miles in width, at such price per acre as may be eventually agreed upon between said Seminole Nation and the party or parties building said road—subject to the approval of the President of the United States: Provided, however, That said land thus sold shall not be reconveyed, leased, or rented to, or be occupied by, any one not a citizen of the Seminole Nation, according to its laws and recognized usages: Provided also, That officers, servants, and employés of said railroad necessary to its construction and management shall not be excluded from such necessary occupancy, they being subject to the provisions of the Indian-intercourse laws, and such rules and regulations as may be established by the Secretary of the Interior; nor shall any conveyance of said lands be made to the party building and managing said road, until its completion as a first-class railroad and its acceptance as such by the Secretary of the Interior.

****

Robert Johnson, his x mark. <————(Freedman)
United States interpreter for Seminole Indians.
Geo. A. Reynolds, United States Indian agent for Seminoles.
Ok-tus-sus-har-jo, his x mark, or Sands.
Cow-e-to-me-ko, his x mark.
Che-chu-chee, his x mark.
Harry Island, his x mark. <————(Freedman)

United States interpreter for Creek Indians.

J. W. Dunn, United States Indian agent for the Creek Nation.

Perry Fuller.

Signed by John F. Brown, special delegate for the Southern Seminoles, in presence of, this June thirtieth, eighteen hundred and sixty-six—

W.R. Irwin.

J. M. Tebbetts.

Geo. A. Reynolds, United States Indian agent.

Robert Johnson, his x mark, United States interpreter.

Glossary

Annuity-Compensation paid for land or resources taken from a tribe. The payments are based on the terms of a treaty or other agreement between the US and the tribe.

Archaic Period-The period of time extending from approximately 6,000 BCE (before the current era) to 1200 BCE. During this time in Florida more diverse habitats were used for hunting, fishing, and gathering. The earliest permanent settlements were established since the search for food required less migration.

Asi (black drink)-A drink made from the plant *ilex vomitoria* that induces vomiting. The black drink was used throughout the Southeastern Indian population for purification rites.

Asi-yohola-The term for the sound made by the individual as the black drink takes affect—the black drink crier.

Bureau of Indian Affairs (BIA)-A US agency established in 1824 and assigned to the Department of the Interior in 1849. Originated to manage trade and other US/Indian relations and to supervise tribes on reservations, now the BIA encourages Indian tribes to manage their own affairs.

Chert-A sedimentary rock formed in Florida. It is limestone that has been replaced by silicon dioxide from clay. It is a hard rock that fractures predictably. Florida Indians used chert for many tools.

Chikkee-An open sided structure built on a raised platform and covered by a thatch roof.

Clan-A multigenerational group of people sharing an identity, organization, and property, based on a belief in a common ancestor. The Seminole clans were determined by matrilineal descent.

Green Corn Dance-Celebration of the harvest of new corn. It is representational of casting out the old and bringing in the new and pure. It is a time for forgiveness and thanksgiving.

Indian Agent-A person appointed by the BIA to supervise US Government programs as to the Indians on a reservation or in a specific geographic area. Post 1908 the term changed to Indian Superintendent.

Indian Removal Act-An 1830 federal law that authorized relocation of the Indians of the East to lands west of the Mississippi River.

Indian Reorganization Act-A 1934 federal law providing for the development of reservation communities.

Matrilineal-Tracing descent through the maternal line.

Medicine Bag or Bundle-A pouch containing spiritual objects used in rituals.

Miccosukee-A tribe of Indians, an offshoot of the Seminoles, a more traditional branch.

Mikasuki-See above.

Paleoindian Period-This is the earliest known period of human habitation in the Americas. Approximately 40,000 BCE to 8,000 BCE.

Pleistocene-The geologic epoch extends from approximately 1.8 million years ago until 10,000 BCE. Also known as the Ice Age.

Reservation-An area of land set aside by treaty for the occupation and use by Indians.

Shaman-A medicine man that uses special powers to call on various spirits to heal the sick and solve day to day problems.

Sofkee-The favored drink of the Seminoles, it is made from mashed corn.

Treaty-A contract negotiated between the US and one or more Indian tribes.

Tribe-A society consisting of many communities united by kinship, clan affiliation, religious, or economic and political institutions. There is usually a common culture and language.

Trust Land-Land set aside and controlled by the US for use by Indians.

Bibliography

For Further Information on the Seminoles

Brown, Robin. *Florida's First People*. Sarasota, Florida, Pineapple Press, 1994.

Colburn, David R., Landers, Jane L. *The African American Heritage of Florida*. Gainesville, Florida, University Press of Florida, 1995.

Foreman, Grant. *The Five Civilized Tribes*, tenth printing. Norman, Oklahoma, University of Oklahoma Press, 1989.

Garbarino, Merwyn S. *The Seminoles: Indians of North America*, Franklin Porter, general editor. New York, New York, Chelsea House Publishers, 1989.

Hakim, Joy. *A History of Us*, Book One. Oxford University Press, 1993.

Jordan, Robert Paul. *The Civil War*, National Geographic Society Senior Editorial Staff. National Geographic Society, 1969.

Kersey, Jr., Harry A. *The Florida Seminoles and the New Deal 1933-1942*. Boca Raton, Florida, Atlantic University Press, 1989.

Mahon, John K. *The History of the Second Seminole War*, revised edition. Gainesville, Florida, University Press of Florida, 1991.

Milanich, Jerald T. *Florida's Indians from Ancient Times to the Present*. Gainesville, Florida, University Press of Florida, 1998.

Paynes Creek State Historic Site Brochure. Bowling Green, Florida.

Porter, Kenneth W. *The Black Seminoles: History of a Freedom Seeking People*, revised and edited Alcione M. Amos and Thomas Senter. Gainesville, Florida, University Press of Florida, 1996.

Schrecengost, Maity. *Panther Girl*. Gainesville, Florida, Maupin House Publishing, Inc., 1999.

Web site of the Seminole Tribe of Florida-*www.seminoletribe.com*

Web site of the Seminole Tribe of Oklahoma-www.cowboy.net/
native/seminole/index.html
www.african-nativeamerican.com/seminole_treaty.htm
www.councilfire.com/treaty/treat108.htm
www.councilfire.com/treaty/treat157.htm
www.patrickjennings-feedback@synaptic.bc.ca

www.ingramcontent.com/pod-product-compliance
Lightning Source LLC
Chambersburg PA
CBHW020246290526
45784CB00003B/1120